SUPPORTING ENGLISH LEARNERS WITH EXCEPTIONAL NEEDS

PATRICIA RICE DORAN
AMY K. NOGGLE
With **GREGORY KNOLLMAN**
HEATHER WAYSON WILSON
JUNE LUCAS ZILLICH

tesol press

This book has a companion website. Go to:
www.tesol.org/exceptionalneeds

www.tesol.org/bookstore

TESOL International Association
1925 Ballenger Avenue
Alexandria, Virginia, 22314 USA
www.tesol.org

Director of Publishing and Product Development: Myrna Jacobs
Copy Editor: Meg Moss
Cover: Citrine Sky Design
Interior Design and Layout: Capitol Communications, LLC
Printing: Gasch Printing, LLC

Copyright © 2019 by TESOL International Association

All rights reserved. Copying or further publication of the contents of this work are not permitted without permission of TESOL International Association, except for limited "fair use" for educational, scholarly, and similar purposes as authorized by U.S. Copyright Law, in which case appropriate notice of the source of the work should be given. Permission to reproduce material from this book must be obtained from www.copyright.com, or contact Copyright Clearance Center, Inc., 222 Rosewood Drive, Danvers, MA 01923, 978-750-8400.

Every effort has been made to contact copyright holders for permission to reprint borrowed material. We regret any oversights that may have occurred and will rectify them in future printings of this work.

ISBN 978-1-945351-23-5
eBook ISBN 978-1-945351-24-2
Library of Congress Control Number 2018963977

CONTENTS

Introduction v

SECTION 1: BACKGROUND KNOWLEDGE

1 **What Do English Learners Bring to Our Schools? Cognitive, Linguistic, and Cultural Assets** 3
Patricia Rice Doran

2 **Challenges and Opportunities for English Learners in Our Schools** 17
June Lucas Zillich, Patricia Rice Doran, and Amy K. Noggle

3 **A Policy Primer** 31
Amy K. Noggle and Gregory Knollman

SECTION 2: CLASSROOM STRUCTURES

4 **Ecological Approaches and Multitiered Systems of Support: Holistic Approaches to Serving English Learners** 49
Patricia Rice Doran and Danielle Turner

5 **Collaborative Problem Solving for English Learners: The Unique Role of the ESOL Teacher** 65
Heather Wayson Wilson

6 **Universal Supports for English Learners at Risk** 79
Patricia Rice Doran and Amy K. Noggle

SECTION 3: SUPPORTS FOR ENGLISH LEARNERS WITH DISABILITIES

7 Targeted Supports for English Learners 97
Patricia Rice Doran and Danielle Turner

**8 Assessment and Identification for English/Culturally and
Linguistically Diverse Learners: High-Incidence Disabilities** 111
Amy K. Noggle and Patricia Rice Doran

**9 Assessment and Identification for English Learners:
Low-Incidence Disabilities** 135
Amy K. Noggle and Patricia Rice Doran

**10 Intensive Supports and Specialized Programming
for English Learners** 147
Patricia Rice Doran and Gregory Knollman

Conclusion 159

INTRODUCTION

To our English learner students, and all culturally and linguistically diverse learners in our schools, their families, and the teachers who serve them.

The US Migration Policy Institute (Park, O'Toole, & Katsiaficas, 2017) indicates that 1 of 10 students in public schools are identified as English learners, and approximately 85% of the youngest of these (pre-K to fifth grade) are native born. A recent study also showed that over 90% of English learner programs still show disparate outcomes for English learners, particularly those with disabilities (Foxen & Mather, 2016). As increasing numbers of schools and classrooms include English learners, increasing numbers of educators are expected to understand second-language acquisition and teach literacy and academic content in languages new to students. In addition, practitioners must consider an added layer: problem solving for those who may have disabilities, a group already established to be at risk in countless studies. At the end of the 2015 school year, the National Center for Education Statistics (NCES) reported that English learners with documented disabilities make up 13.8% of the total EL population in our nation's K–12 schools (NCES, 2017). These facts, together, suggest that it is increasingly important for educators to be familiar with the needs of English learners, as they include a growing portion of our students; that English to Speakers of Other Languages (ESOL) and other specialized programs may be necessary but not sufficient to meet the needs of this growing group of students; and that all educators must rise to the challenge of addressing the double risk factors of language learning and disability that may impact these students.

These seeming challenges also present extraordinary opportunities to school personnel and to the entire educational system; in making needed changes to support English learners, all of us have the opportunity to reevaluate practice and improve our day-to-day work with diverse learners. At the same time, these efforts to improve daily practice are urgent, as achievement and opportunity gaps continue to affect scores of English learners, particularly those who are already at risk in terms of academics or behavior. Our children come to school with a wealth of information that stems from family, culture, and language. They come with beautiful curiosity and a desire to belong, learn, and succeed. It is our collective responsibility, working within an ecological framework, to support the whole child, academically and socioemotionally. Doing so effectively will allow us to change the trajectories of our English learners who have specific learning needs.

This book grew out of the urgency surrounding those trajectories; English learners with disabilities often have tremendous potential but remain underserved in our schools, as demonstrated by national data. Some core theories undergird our work: Carol Dweck's (2007) examination of growth mindset, theories of equity and cultural responsiveness, the whole-child framework, and the Universal Design for Learning approach. These theories are not specific to ESOL or the field of second-language acquisition in general; rather, our emphasis in this book is developmental, and our goal is to situate the cultural and linguistic needs of English learners within the whole-child, developmental perspective essential to special education.

In our discussions of this topic, over several years of collaboration, on this and other projects, we returned again and again to the core belief that effective supports for English learners with disabilities begin long before the point of identification and individual education program (IEP) development. In fact, effective supports and services for English learners with disabilities cannot exist outside a school structure dedicated to the success of all learners, at every tier of instruction. It may seem counterintuitive for a book addressing programming and supports for English learners with disabilities to spend the first five chapters addressing topics such as developmental assets and universally designed instruction. In today's schools, though, much of our service delivery for students with disabilities occurs—as it should—informally (through response-to-intervention approaches), inclusively (in general education settings), and collaboratively (with the involvement of multiple professionals in varied roles). Specialized interventions and programming are often the culminating steps in a process of inclusive, linguistically responsive instruction that should begin with the first encounter between a student's family and the school system. We further believe—and evidence has shown—that specialized interventions and programming have a much higher likelihood of success when they occur in conjunction with strong problem-solving processes at all levels, inclusive approaches to education, and a commitment to appropriate special education identification. For that reason, our final few chapters provide in-depth discussion of topics traditionally associated with "special education": formal assessment, family involvement in decision-making, and individualized education planning. These chapters are preceded in the book, as they must be in practice, by extensive discussion of strengths-based and deficit-based mindsets (so that we do not mistakenly assume children's differences are disabilities), collaborative problem solving (so that we ensure all professionals with appropriate expertise are involved in supporting any given child), and universal supports for curriculum access (so that English learners with disabilities can thrive, when possible, in general education classrooms as they access the general education curriculum).

This book is designed to be practitioner-friendly and easy to read. Each chapter includes real-life vignettes, discussion of key concepts, practical approaches and strategies, and reflection or discussion questions. There is also a companion website rich with resources: www.tesol.org/exceptionalneeds. We hope these resources will deepen and improve practices, offering teachers and school leaders a set of classroom-ready tools and ideas relevant to their English learners who may have disabilities.

Section 1 covers foundational background knowledge related to English learners. In chapter 1, we present a strengths-based approach to English learners, an alternative to the popular and insidious deficit-based methods of considering these students and their abilities. Chapter 2, by June Lucas Zillich, Patricia Rice Doran, and Amy Noggle, describes some of the needs this unique group of students may bring to school, highlighting the opportunities these needs, and students' abilities, can present for schools and teachers. In chapter 3, Noggle and Gregory Knollman present an overview of policies that affect English learners, policies that affect children with disabilities, and how these laws often intersect in day-to-day practice.

Section 2 describes the structures present in responsive, culturally sustaining schools and classrooms. Chapter 4, by Rice Doran and Danielle Turner, describes ecological frameworks and discusses their importance for English learners in particular; in chapter 5, Heather Wayson Wilson identifies and discusses key elements of responsive problem-solving protocols and intrastaff collaboration, a key practice for supporting English learners with and without disabilities. And in chapter 6, Rice Doran and Noggle review the fundamentals of UDL and its importance in foundational classroom instruction for English learners.

Section 3 addresses targeted and intensive supports for English learners with (or at risk for) disabilities and presents strategies and recommended practices for assessment, identification, and IEP development for this important group of students. In chapter 7, Rice Doran describes targeted supports and response-to-intervention practices for English learners with academic or behavioral needs. Chapters 8 and 9, both by Noggle and Rice Doran, describe recommended assessment and identification practices for English learners who may have high-incidence disabilities and those with low-incidence disabilities, respectively. Finally, in chapter 10, Rice Doran and Knollman review considerations for intensive supports and service delivery for students following identification and IEP development. This chapter ends our book—but we hope that, along with the preceding chapters, it serves as a beginning point for readers in reflecting on, and continuously improving, their services and supports for English learners with and without disabilities.

Like all collaborative enterprises, this book has benefited greatly from the time, talents, and inspiration of many individuals who may not be listed in references throughout the text but whose support has been invaluable in the development and refinement of these concepts. In particular, we are grateful to our colleagues at Arcola Elementary School in Montgomery County Public Schools in Maryland, including the school's dedicated principal, Emmanuel Jean-Phillippe, and assistant principal, Jessica Blasic. We have also learned from the valuable work of the

Montgomery County Linkages to Learning Program–Community School Initiative, which incorporates innovative thinking within critical partnerships in the district. We are also indebted to our colleagues at Towson University, including our ever-supportive chair, Betsy Neville, and Gilda Martinez-Alba, whose encouragement in the early stages of this project was critical. We have gained inspiration from countless students and teachers over the years, particularly those with whom we have worked in our capacity as instructors, researchers, and school and central office administrators. And we are forever indebted to our family members: Bill, Bryce, Grant, and Hope Noggle; Robert, Sam, and Felix Wilson; Chad, James, Claire, Katie, Julia, Conor and Mary Doran; and Phil, Anna, Phil Jr., Winston, Daniel, and Clementine Turner. Last, but certainly not least, our competent and supportive editor at TESOL Press, Myrna Jacobs, has provided invaluable feedback every step of the way. We are tremendously appreciative to her; her assistant Kari Dalton; our copy editor, Meg Moss; David Cutler, TESOL's Policy Manager, who provided expert advice, and to all of the dedicated and talented publishing council members, staff, and reviewers at TESOL Press who have worked to bring this project to fruition.

References

Dweck, C. (2007). *Mindset: The new psychology of success*. New York: Ballantine.

Foxen, P., & Mather, M. (2016). Toward a more equitable future—The trends and challenges facing America's Latino children. Retrieved from http://publications.unidosus.org/handle/123456789/1627

National Center for Education Statistics. (2018). English language learners in public schools. Retrieved from http://nces.ed.gov/programs/coe/ indicator_cgf.asp

Park, M., O'Toole, A., & Katsiaficas, C. (2017). Dual language learners: A national demographic and policy profile. Washington, DC: Migration Policy Institute. Retrieved from https://www.migrationpolicy.org/research/dual-language-learners-national-demographic-and-policy-profile

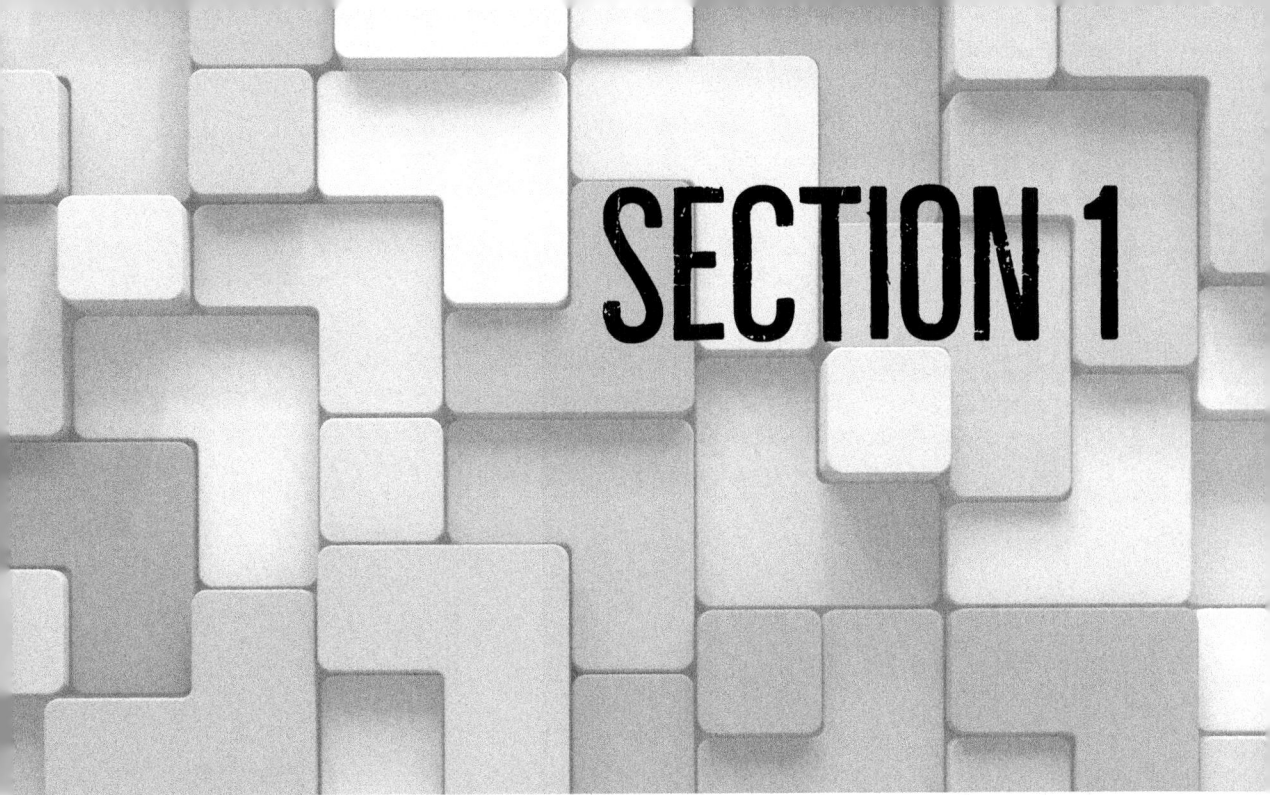

SECTION 1

BACKGROUND KNOWLEDGE

CHAPTER 1

WHAT DO ENGLISH LEARNERS BRING TO OUR SCHOOLS? COGNITIVE, LINGUISTIC, AND CULTURAL ASSETS

PATRICIA RICE DORAN

Sebastian's Journey

Sebastian is an 11-year-old student who had crossed the southern border of the United States the previous year with his mother, cousins, and older brother. Traveling without documentation, Sebastian and his family took a circuitous route to their current home in the Midwest, where they have distant relatives. Sebastian began sixth grade at a large middle school with ESOL services and a transitional 1-year program for students with interrupted education. Sebastian's teachers in this transitional program report that he is eager to please, yet has difficulty focusing and completing work. As they worked to address his language needs and deficits in content knowledge, one of his teachers also noticed he is particularly adept in two areas: connecting with peers and problem solving in practical situations. In fact, when the power went out unexpectedly, Sebastian was the first student in the class to pipe up with a suggestion for continuing the lesson. When a classmate joked about wanting to learn how to play golf, Sebastian googled the sport and created a set of miniature golf balls and a club, using loose-leaf paper and tape. Sebastian's teachers use these observations to modify how they present lessons to Sebastian and how they differentiate products for him. During partner work, they make sure to give Sebastian and his partner practical tasks with concrete deliverables (such as a chart, a sculpture, or a model). In math instruction, they include at least three practical, real-world problems in each lesson—two for the teacher and class to solve, and one for students to work on during independent practice. These strategies, they find, not only help to engage Sebastian more, but also allow him to master content at a faster rate. Most of all, his teachers find they are better able to appreciate Sebastian as a person, taking into account his strengths rather than focusing on his deficits.

Frequently, we see our culturally and linguistically diverse (CLD) learners through a deficit lens, noting what they can't do (speak English fluently), haven't mastered (demands of academic language), and aren't familiar with (daily school routines). Doing this constitutes a great injustice not only to these students but to the rest of our students as well. In fact, CLD learners bring tremendous assets to schools, enriching not only their own learning but also that of peers. Appropriately identifying and leveraging these strengths is a critical component of good practice. This chapter describes the evidence base underlying these strengths, provides practical strategies for utilizing strengths of learners who are CLD or English learners, and places strengths-based teaching in the context of overall responsive practice and identification for this population.

In a book addressing comprehensive supports for English learners with disabilities, it may seem unusual to begin with a general look at this population's strengths. Indeed, educators often view disabilities through a lens focused on deficits and challenges (Harry & Klingner, 2007) rather than on assets. Serving English learners with disabilities can be challenging precisely because our system is not built to take account, or advantage, of their unique strengths and gifts. These strengths may provide students notable resilience or socioemotional skills; may manifest in culturally unexpected or underappreciated ways; and may mask the impact of existing disabilities, further complicating the assessment and identification process. For all of these reasons, it is essential to begin by understanding the unique attributes—including strengths as well as needs—that our English learners bring to our schools, particularly when those students may be candidates for special education services.

Additionally, a strengths-based approach is fundamental to special education, philosophically and practically. In recent years, special education has increasingly emphasized students' strengths and abilities alongside their needs for additional support (Armstrong, 2012). Helping students to achieve to their greatest abilities is possible only when we accurately understand what those abilities are. Understanding students' current skills and abilities, and areas where they excel, also allows school personnel to set realistic yet challenging goals to maximize their potential (Climie & Henley, 2016).

What does it mean in practice to consider students' strengths, along with their needs? The story of Sebastian at the start of this chapter provides an example. Sebastian's teachers leveraged several assets he brought with him into the classroom, including his resilience, his social skills and peer relationships, and his native language abilities. Various frameworks and concepts can help us to identify assets such as these. Some, such as a list of developmental assets, are more structured, while others, such as strengths-based language, may be less formalized. The following section reviews several of the most frequently used frameworks and concepts as a starting point.

Important Concepts for Strengths-Based Viewing of English Learners

While careful and responsive differentiation for each student is essential, commonalities often exist in the concepts schools and teachers may leverage to support English learners' achievements through their unique abilities. Each of these concepts is listed, then described briefly and discussed in more detail as it relates to specific students' needs. Throughout the rest of this book, as we discuss planning for instructional and socioemotional needs, these concepts will serve as reference and starting points for strengths-based intervention.

Positive vs. deficit-based language. Sometimes, it is tempting to describe students' challenges in a sort of shorthand, focusing on what they cannot do or the competencies they lack. Even in describing genuine needs that students bring to the classroom, educators provide a better roadmap forward for problem solving when they lead with what students can do instead of what they cannot (Harry & Klingner, 2007). This idea is hardly new; Harry and Klingner (2007) cite a 1983 article that describes dramatic gaps between the narrative skills that African American students actually had and the skills their teachers assumed they had (Brice-Heath, 1983). In formulating statements such as, "Josefina cannot add," or "Martin doesn't ever pay attention," teachers run the risk of overstating challenges and eliminating the nuance and additional information that could be teased out through careful description. In fact, you can gather a great deal more information from more careful, nuanced statements such as: "When given a set of single-digit numbers, Josefina can add successfully if she is provided extra time; however, she is not successful in adding double-digit numbers even with extra time." Such a statement not only allows the teacher to hypothesize exactly where Josefina is experiencing difficulty (making the transition from single-digit to double-digit addition), but it also suggests some potential accommodations and interventions (targeted support with double-digit addition; extra time once that targeted support has been provided). Table 1 lists some frequently used "deficit words" and phrases and suggests alternatives.

Table 1 **Deficit-Oriented Phrases and Suggested Alternatives**

Frequent deficit phrase	**Alternatives**
Does not	Can _____ but has not demonstrated ability to _____
Will not	Does _____ on a regular basis but does not do _____ on a regular basis
Refuses to/Chooses not to	Does _____ on a regular basis but does not do _____ on a regular basis
Unmotivated	Does complete _____ tasks but does not complete _____ tasks on a regular basis
Lazy	Does engage in _____ tasks but does not engage in _____ tasks

Developmental approaches to growth and disability. It is also easy to look at development and disability themselves through a deficit-focused lens. Of necessity, special education requires identification of specific deficits, and individualized education programs (IEPs) typically describe extensively what challenges and needs students demonstrate. In recent years, the adoption of response-to-intervention (RTI) and multitiered systems of support (MTSS) paradigms have encouraged educators to take a holistic and developmental approach toward student needs, providing interventions and supports as indicated without the need for specific labels or diagnoses (NCCREST, 2008; National Center on Response to Intervention, 2011) and meeting students at their current levels of performance and achievement while considering how best to support their growth. It should be noted, and will be discussed later in this text in more depth, that the use of an RTI/MTSS model should not limit intensive, early intervention for those students who truly need it; when data identify a student as significantly at-risk, intensive supports can and should be implemented promptly (Fuchs & Vaughn, 2012).

Responsive, individualized approaches are particularly important for English learners, who may present with uneven skills in some areas, particularly those relating to language and cultural familiarity. These students may appear advanced in some skills or domains, such as creativity, problem solving, or ability to adapt and transition. They may likewise appear to be challenged in other areas, particularly those related to formal academic knowledge that may not have been part of their prior educational experiences.

Furthermore, even for students who are not English learners, the continuum of development must be taken into account. Particularly in the early childhood years, students may develop at different rates, leading to potential mismatches between their achievement and their teachers' expectations. Several recent studies, for example, have found that students who are the youngest in their grades have a significantly higher likelihood of being diagnosed with ADHD (Chen et al., 2016; Morrow et al., 2012). These studies, and some additional literature (Thomas, Mitchell, & Batstra, 2013; Cohen, Hockman, & Bedard, 2017), suggest that, for some students, the issue is less one of their intrinsic abilities and more one of developmental pace matching the expectations their environment and their teachers place on them. Anecdotally, our experience bears this out. It is not uncommon, in student problem-solving meetings, to hear staff express concerns about a kindergarten student who turns out to be one of the younger in their grade. Some clinicians in our experience have recommended "the tincture of time" for students experiencing regression or delayed development, rather than beginning more intensive treatment. It is, granted, sometimes a fine line between watchful waiting and proactive intervention. Carefully evaluating a student's current level of functioning can help teams to make this decision wisely (see Table 2).

Table 2   Developmental Considerations: When to Intervene and When to Wait

How far behind peers is the student?

Is the student evidencing a rate of growth that will lead to improvements?

Is the student showing signs of frustration, social isolation, or depression?

Are the student's parents significantly concerned?

Are the student's skills impacting participation in curriculum or activities?

See the story of Rivka at www.tesol.org/exceptionalneeds for a useful illustration of how teachers and teams might balance developmental awareness with carefully chosen, proactive supports. Developmental approaches often require a careful balance on the part of teachers, who need to remain vigilant without rushing to judgment or inappropriately referring for more intensive intervention than might be appropriate. As discussed below, looking at a child through a developmental lens also requires consideration of their strengths. The concept of developmental assets can be particularly helpful here.

Developmental assets. The Developmental Assets Framework (Search Institute, 2015) suggests that children can draw upon preexisting developmental assets and benefits from their backgrounds. The Developmental Assets Framework (which can be found on the Search Institute website at http://page.search-institute.org/40-developmental-assets) comprises "40 research-based, positive experiences" that build students' skills, resilience, and abilities to "help them become positive, caring adults" (Search Institute, 2015). Over the past three decades, the Developmental Assets Framework has been refined to include focus on key relationships and community attributes that can also support growth in students and to incorporate elements from extensive research (Scales & Leffert, 1999). While the entire list of assets is available through the Search Institute, a few are referenced here to illustrate the value of considering assets that students may have developed in their personal (or school) experiences and that may influence their classroom performance.

This particular organization's list of developmental assets is not tailored to English learners specifically. However, considering existing strengths and assets students have acquired (as a general practice) and considering this framework of Developmental Assets (in particular) can have striking relevance to English learners. In looking at the list of Developmental Assets for adolescents, as one example, it is striking that many of these assets, which are linked to positive growth and maturity in young people, are related to attributes that some English learners develop as a result of life experiences. Traits such as "personal responsibility," "cultural competence" (comfort with individuals from different cultures and ease in navigating cultural differences with sensitivity), and "planning ahead" are listed as developmental assets (Search Institute, 2015). Both anecdotes and research bear out the multiple ways English learners often demonstrate responsibility, planning, and sociocultural competence beyond their years, and planning with these unique abilities in mind supports student achievement (Willner & Monroe, 2016). It is also important to note that such traits are often culturally mediated in the ways they are displayed; teams may overlook students' personal responsibility, or caring family members, if they are using a lens that does not account for the different ways students may demonstrate responsibility or caring in differing cultural and family contexts. Indeed, as English learners are particularly vulnerable to family separation, it is important for school personnel to keep in mind that family relationships may take a variety of forms that may or may not be immediately evident to school personnel. Alfredo, for example, lives with a cousin but communicates nightly with his mother, Luisa, who is still in Honduras, via Skype, phone, or messaging app. While geographically distant, Luisa has recently given Alfredo advice on everything from choosing a research paper topic to how to ask his boss for more hours at work. Her involvement and care might not be evident to Alfredo's teachers unless they are quite familiar with his life outside school. While physically distant, Luisa has proven to be an invaluable developmental asset for Alfredo.

The story of Rihanna, which can be found at www.tesol.org/exceptionalneeds, describes additional ways teams can utilize developmental assets in planning using a culturally sensitive lens.

Funds of knowledge from self, family, and community. The "funds of knowledge" approach has potential to transform our traditional, deficit-based views of diverse students. Often, these students bring with them complex cognitive, social, and academic skills, even if they did not develop them in traditional English-speaking school settings. These may differ in significant ways from cultural and developmental expectations placed on American students. For example, a student in middle school may exercise far greater level of responsibility in his family environment than a typical American middle-schooler might, supporting younger siblings with homework, taking the lead on dinner preparation, and even making grocery lists, shopping, or paying bills. Educators often think of such responsibilities in terms of their drawbacks—they may distract students from homework or keep them from attending after-school activities. However, those activities also provide students with a rich reservoir of real-world knowledge and skills, including budgeting, practical and applied mathematics, interpersonal skills, and development of personal responsibility. Traditional academic assessments may not reflect such skills, and teachers may find their diverse learners at risk for poor school performance or special education referral. However, a funds of knowledge approach can help educators to focus on the nontraditional, authentic ways students may be leveraging their skills, and this can be a first step to helping students utilize those skills in school settings as well. The story of Alphonse, at www.tesol.org/exceptionalneeds, illustrates the potential of seeing students through a lens focused on their funds of knowledge.

Language, culture, and resilience: Additional and essential assets. Bilingual or bidialectical students often demonstrate sophisticated social competency in their ability to code-switch, or utilize different forms of language or dialect in social situations when each is called for (Pandey, 2012). Teachers may notice English learners in schools utilizing one form of language or dialect with peers in social settings and another form in school, in their community with parents or elders, or in church or work settings. To do so demonstrates social competence, understanding of various contexts socially and cognitively, and adaptability in language use. Addressing the needs of English learners in a comprehensive, strengths-based context requires educators, first and foremost, to see this language diversity not as a deficit to be remedied but as a profound asset—even if it presents a corresponding challenge for students in accessing monolingual classroom instruction.

Similarly, educators may think of students' life challenges and experiences as potential deficits, but these often serve as opportunities to develop remarkable resilience. The American Psychological Association defines *resilience* as "the process of adapting well in the face of adversity, trauma, tragedy, threats, or significant sources of stress" (APA, n.d.). As students demonstrate this ability to adapt, they benefit from specific approaches such as supportive connections, encouragement to pursue their goals, and social support (APA, n.d.). Teachers and school personnel can play a critical role in supporting their English learners who are experiencing stress, adversity, or trauma both by being aware of students' changing life circumstances and being open to hearing families' stories. As students who have experienced stress or trauma may bring real and intensive needs to the classroom, teachers may also rely on their positive relationships with students and their positive views of students' abilities as they connect students to additional needed supports.

One teacher of our acquaintance recently shared a story about a third-grader in her classroom who had crossed into the United States, without legal documentation, accompanied by his uncle. His uncle had subsequently died on the trip, and the student, taken in by a new family, walked from the southern border to a temporary home several hundred miles away. When he began school in the United States, this student was unquestionably in need of a variety of services, including counseling as well as ESOL. More important, though, the student arrived in school having already demonstrated resilience far beyond those typical of third-graders raised in the United States without unusual circumstances. His teachers' challenge is to accurately assess his functioning to ensure he receives appropriate supports, but also to value his resilience and adaptability, considering those as positive attributes and including those in their estimates of his overall abilities and strengths. At times, this also means overlooking some challenging behaviors, as long as they do not pose a threat to student safety or well-being, with the understanding that some behavioral difficulty might occur as the student adjusts to his new life and the demands of his new school environment. The support of the school counselor, who provided the student a timetable for breaks and a "safe space" in which to take them, is invaluable in this regard. Both counselor and classroom teachers make sure to praise the student frequently for appropriate behavior, persistence, and creativity in the classroom, continuing to build on existing skills. In a less responsive school setting, this student might be frequently disciplined and labeled as "disruptive," without having a chance to demonstrate his true abilities or have his strengths appropriately valued.

Educators must be aware of students' levels of resilience and emotional strength, not only to leverage them when appropriate, but also to avoid placing additional undue stress on students who may still be processing difficult or traumatic events in their home countries or in the United States. Borjian (2016) recounts the story of a student without documentation who succeeded in the US educational system and went to a 4-year college, describing both the student's resilience and the supportive efforts of educators who worked with her. Culturally and linguistically responsive teaching strategies were central to this student's success and to others, as they provide ways to connect with her heritage and prior experiences and also to build bridges to future learning. Awareness of students' needs and resilience can be helpful to all school personnel in supporting those students' academic and socioemotional growth (Liebenberg et al., 2016).

Practical Application

With these assets in mind, then, let's return to the scenario of Sebastian from the beginning of the chapter. Sebastian's teachers have leveraged his strengths and skills in helping him continue to achieve. If we look specifically at the areas discussed above, Sebastian has benefited from teachers' awareness and willingness to build on the following:

- **Developmental assets:** His relationships with family; presence of supportive adults in his life; personal skills in multiple areas
- **Strengths:** His problem-solving skills, peer relationships
- **Funds of knowledge:** His tactile and practical problem-solving abilities; real-world applications and knowledge gained from family members; interpersonal skills developed in family and community

- **Linguistic and cultural assets and resilience:** His ability to shift between his native language and English in social or academic situations; ability to cultivate positive relationships with adults; being eager to please and receptive to advice; ability to successfully adapt to changes and stressors, whether academic, social, or community-based

In a different school, with different teachers, Sebastian might very well have been identified as a "struggling learner" with limited potential for achievement. However, his teachers' awareness of his gifts, along with his instructional and linguistic needs, allowed them to plan a tailored set of supports to help him succeed. In schools and classrooms where such differentiation occurs, multiple factors often underlie these successful efforts. This type of differentiation and responsive planning is critical for appropriate support of English learners, including those who may have disabilities, so that their special education plans can be formulated with their strengths as well as needs in mind. Additionally, and equally important, such differentiation early in a student's educational career can put them on a successful trajectory and reduce the need for intensive supports and specialized programming in later years.

Let's look quickly at the characteristics of his school, classroom, and family involvement paradigm that have allowed Sebastian to thrive.

Schoolwide valuation of student strengths and assets: What practices can school leaders use? Literature suggests that when schools value students' cultural and developmental assets, this can be a powerful influence for positive outcomes (Simcox, Nuijens, & Lee, 2006). In our experience, schools that value students' unique assets often share the following traits.

Multilingual staff and materials. Having staff members who can speak the various languages at your school—beyond the one or two that are most represented—makes a powerful if implicit statement to families that their backgrounds and opinions are valued. Similarly, the time needed to translate resources and notes home, or secure interpreters for all meetings, often pays off by cementing bonds with families who are included far more in the school's daily activities than they might be in an English-only communications system.

Positive messaging about students and families. This may take the form of posters on the walls, greetings at the beginning of the day, friendly and affirming language in newsletters, and class discussions and events allowing students to see families and schools interact.

Variety of events welcoming a variety of students and families. Often, events move beyond the traditional "bring food from your culture" night and embrace more complex topics such as reading night, health-education night, middle school (or college) preparation night, and so on.

Educational outreach for families as well as students. Outreach to families about continuing education may allow parents and family members to build on their unique skills and background experiences and continue to develop them. These might include English classes, literacy classes, family exercise events or classes, and GED preparation.

Variety of supports available for students/families. In responsive schools, these often involve connecting families with each other and leveraging families' positive attributes, through peer educators, community liaisons, and family support groups.

Twelve-month programming. Year-round initiatives such as summer school and summer workshops for families allow students, and their relatives, to continue developing their knowledge and skills beyond the academic year.

Community connections with local agencies, food pantries, tutoring services, nonprofits, and businesses (for philanthropic support and job opportunities for students). Such connections may take time for school leaders or family support coordinators to build, but they can pay extensive dividends for both students and families.

Classroom valuation of student strengths and assets: What practices can classroom teachers support? In addition to schoolwide frameworks and practices, individual teachers can bring about positive results for their students by incorporating strengths-based, culturally sensitive approaches in their instruction and intervention processes. Suggestions for teacher practices and strategies follow.

Appropriate use of prereferral steps. Appropriate prereferral practices may include referring a student to a team consideration process, rather than initiating special education referral, if the student is struggling, along with trying classroom-level interventions and strategies. Conversely, as data indicate more intensive needs on the student's part, more immediate action and referral may be indicated sooner. Flexibility, and adapting the process to each individual student's needs, both play a key role here.

Positive classroom talk. Affirming messages—both explicit and implicit—help students capitalize on their abilities and skills. These messages may include specific praise for tasks done well or general affirmations. ("This test is hard, but I have confidence in you all.") Keep in mind that research finds that praise is most meaningful when it is concrete, tied to a specific experience, reinforcing desired academic-success behaviors, and authentic. ("I like the way you persevered on that problem" is more meaningful than "You all are so smart!" or "Great effort!") (Dweck, 2012).

Frequent use of oral language. Providing a classroom environment rich in oral language helps to accelerate student mastery of language proficiency and oral literacy standards.

Frequent reference to diverse cultures and communities. Incorporating diverse backgrounds, practices, and family experiences into instruction without fanfare helps students to appreciate the wide range of backgrounds and experiences their classmates may have.

Anchoring new learning goals to students' current skills and proficiencies. Building on prior knowledge is a recognized brain-friendly practice (Willis, 2007). This includes tying new learning goals to prior knowledge gained in a different language to maximize students' linguistic and cognitive abilities (Cummins, 2007).

Experiential learning opportunities. Tying learning activities to authentic, real-world experiences, especially those based in the community, helps to build students' social and communicative competence, increases the implicit value the school places on what the community should offer, and leverages prior knowledge and motivation.

Involving family and communities: What practices can schools and teachers support?
While family involvement is often one of the last things discussed in supporting student needs, its role is among the most critical. Children with involved families are more successful in school, both socially and academically (Noel, Stark, Redford, & Zukerberg, 2016). Research suggests that the role of meaningful family involvement in school may be even more important for children with disabilities, as they are at a greater risk for adverse academic, social, and behavioral outcomes. Throughout this book, family involvement strategies and recommendations are integrated into each chapter and topic, on the assumption that continued partnership with families is essential at all stages of the support, planning and differentiation, and interventions process—not just while writing the final individualized educational program. However, in practice, both school leaders and teachers may find it difficult to contact families of English learners and to support their needs in an appropriate, responsive, and effective manner. Here are a few recommendations to get started.

Clear communication with families. Communicating clearly with families involves, first, ensuring communication occurs in a mutually intelligible language or supports are provided for mutual intelligibility. Defining terms and educational jargon, so all parties have equivalent understanding, is also important. Finally, both school leaders and teachers should consider the manner and frequency of communication. Is it frequent enough? Is it presented in a readily available and accessible format? Is it detailed enough, or too detailed?

Asking good questions about what students know. Implementing a strengths-based approach relies, first of all, on accurately assessing and understanding students' strengths. To do this, teachers must have a clear indication of what students know and can do. To accomplish this, they should utilize appropriate questioning strategies, evaluate prior knowledge (in multiple languages if called for), and provide students opportunities to show their knowledge using multiple modalities and means of expression (CAST, 2011).

Nonthreatening interactions with families. As political climates change, particularly with respect to immigration enforcement, families may hold varying perceptions about the role of schools and their interactions with school personnel. Sadly, immigrant families who fear deportation may be very reluctant to become involved in school-based activities (McWayne, Campos, & Owsianik, 2008). Explicitly reassuring families as to their children's safety and access to education may be helpful; clarification about local, state, and federal enforcement actions may be appropriate as family questions arise. For example, if families have questions about whether immigration enforcement actions can occur at school events, it may be helpful for school or district leadership to clarify as needed.

Explicitly valuing families' experiences, cultures, and backgrounds. When opportunities present themselves, school staff should express the ways in which they value families' diversity, both generally and in specific circumstances. This might include mentioning and affirming all of the various nationalities represented in a school community during back-to-school night; it might also include commenting on particular ways family and cultural background enriches a student's experience: "We're so glad he has the opportunity to return to Honduras to visit his grandmother. What a great experience that will be. We'll make sure his makeup work is ready for him when he gets back."

Strengths-based approaches incorporated into problem solving and remediation. Responsive instruction and positive school environments can mitigate and prevent many problems. However, schools will still have students who require additional targeted or intensive supports. Strengths-based thinking can play an important role here as well. As with Sebastian, any problem-solving process should begin with an inventory of what a student does well and how those attributes or skills might be leveraged to help them improve in areas of need. Further elements of problem-solving will be described in later chapters of this book and, therefore, are not addressed in detail here.

Summary and Conclusion

The remainder of this book deals in greater depth with questions of how to provide effective interventions, assessments, and programming for English learners with exceptionalities. In our view, this chapter forms an essential prelude to such discussions. As with any population of students, English learners are best served within a holistic context that affirms their unique gifts even as it provides structured, deliberately chosen supports to help them attain proficiency. Such a program furthers the cause of educational equity, as English learners who receive an accessible, appropriate education are well positioned for a variety of successful postsecondary outcomes.

Questions for Team Discussion or Shared Reflection

1. How familiar is our school staff with concepts such as strengths-based thinking, funds of knowledge, and student resilience? Are there ways we can explicitly build one another's knowledge in these areas?
2. Have we utilized strengths-based language in conceptualizing students' needs, or do we still speak in words that reflect deficit-based assumptions? If the latter, how can we reframe our language and thinking?
3. How does our school value students' many strengths and assets? Are these assets valued at the schoolwide level, in individual classrooms, and throughout the problem-solving process?

References

Armstrong, T. (2012). *Neurodiversity in the classroom: Strength-based strategies to help students with special needs succeed in school and life.* Alexandria, VA: ASCD, 2012.

Bialystok, E. (2011). Reshaping the mind: The benefits of bilingualism. *Canadian Journal of Expert Psychology, 65*(4), 229–235. doi:10.1037/a00025406

Borjian, A. (2016). Educational resilience of an undocumented immigrant student: Educators as bridge makers. *CATESOL Journal, 28*(2), 121–139.

Brice-Heath, S. (1983). *Ways with words: Language, life, and work in communities and classrooms.* Cambridge, MA: Cambridge University Press.

CAST (2011). *Universal Design for Learning Guidelines version 2.0.* Retrieved from http://www.udlcenter.org/aboutudl/udlguidelines/principle2

Chen, M., Lan, W., Bai, Y., Huang, K., Su, T., Tsai, S., . . .Hsu, J. (2016). Influence of relative age on diagnosis and treatment of attention-deficit/hyperactivity disorder in Taiwanese children. *Journal of Pediatrics, 172*(May), 162–167.

Climie, E., & Henley, L. (2016). A renewed focus on strengths-based assessment in schools. *British Journal of Special Education, 43*(2), 108–121.

Cohen, P., Hockman, M., & Bedard, P. (2017). Is ADHD overdiagnosed and overtreated? [Blog post]. Retrieved from http://www.health.harvard.edu/blog/is-adhd-overdiagnosed-and-overtreated-2017031611304

Cummins, J. (2007). Rethinking monolingual instructional strategies in multilingual classrooms. *Canadian Journal of Applied Linguistics/Revue canadienne de linguistique appliquée, 10*(2), 221–240.

Dweck, C. (2012). *Mindset: Changing the way you think to fulfill your potential.* London: Hachette.

Esteban-Guitart, M., & Moll, L. C. (2014). Funds of identity: A new concept based on the funds of knowledge approach. *Culture & Psychology, 20*(1), 31–48.

Fuchs, L. S., & Vaughn, S. (2012). Responsiveness-to-intervention: A decade later. *Journal of Learning Disabilities, 45*(3), 195–203. http://doi.org/10.1177/0022219412442150

Harry, B. & Klingner, J. (2007). Discarding the deficit model. *Educational Leadership, 64*(5), 16–21.

Liebenberg, L., Theron, L., Sanders, J., Munford, R., van Rensburg, A., Rothmann, S., & Ungar, M. (2016). Bolstering resilience through teacher-student interaction: Lessons for school psychologists. *School Psychology International, 37*(2), 140–154.

McWayne, C., Campos, R., & Owsianik, M. (2008). A multidimensional, multilevel examination of mother and father involvement among culturally diverse Head Start families. *Journal of School Psychology, 46*(5), 551–573.

Moll, L. C., Amanti, C., Neff, D., & Gonzalez, N. (1992). Funds of knowledge for teaching: Using a qualitative approach to connect homes and classrooms. *Theory into Practice, 31*(2), 132–141.

Morrow, R., Garland, J., Wright, J., Maclure, M., Taylor, S., & Dormuth, C. (2012). Influence of relative age on diagnosis and treatment of attention-deficit hyperactivity disorder in children. *Canadian Medical Association Journal, 184*(7), 162–167. doi:10.1503/cmaj.111619

National Center for Culturally Responsive Educational Systems. (2008). Retrieved from https://rti4success.org/resource/culturally-responsive-response-intervention

National Center on Response to Intervention (2011). *RTI considerations for English language learners (ELLs)*. Washington, DC: US Department of Education, Office of Special Education Programs, National Center on Response to Intervention.

Noel, A., Stark, P., Redford, J., & Zukerberg, A. (2016). Parent and family involvement in education, from the NHES survey of 2012. Retrieved from https://nces.ed.gov/pubs2013/2013028rev.pdf

Pandey, A. (2012). *Language building blocks: Essential linguistics for early childhood educators.* New York, NY: Teachers' College Press.

Scales, P. C., & Leffert, N. (1999). *Developmental assets: A synthesis of the scientific research on adolescent development.* Minneapolis, MN: Search Institute.

Search Institute. (2015). What we study: Developmental Assets. Retrieved from http://www.search-institute.org/what-we-study/developmental-assets

Simcox, A., Nuijens, K., & Lee, C. (2006). School counselors and school psychologists: Collaborative partners in promoting culturally competent schools. *Professional School Counseling, 9*(4), 272–277.

Thomas, R., Mitchell, G., & Batstra, L. (2013). Attention-deficit/hyperactivity disorder: Are we helping or harming? *British Medical Journal, 347*. doi:https://doi.org/10.1136/bmj.f6172

Willis, J. (2007). Brain-friendly strategies for the inclusion classroom. Alexandria, VA: ASCD.

Willner, L. & Monroe, M. (2016). Using a "can-do" approach to ensure differentiated instruction intentionally supports the needs of language learners. Retrieved from http://www.colorincolorado.org/article/using-can-do-approach-ensure-differentiated-instruction-intentionally-supports-needs

Zeichner, K., Payne, K. A., & Brayko, K. (2015). Democratizing teacher education. *Journal of Teacher Education, 66*(2), 122–135.

CHAPTER 2

CHALLENGES AND OPPORTUNITIES FOR ENGLISH LEARNERS IN OUR SCHOOLS

JUNE LUCAS ZILLICH, PATRICIA RICE DORAN, AND AMY NOGGLE

Opportunities for Isabel

Isabel, an English learner who recently arrived from Honduras, is a 12-year-old student who has been attending class for a little over a month. She is designated as a Level 1 (beginner) student in ESOL. She arrived through the district's International Office, with some noted educational interruption in her background. Her file indicates that Isabel had been attending school in her home country, but did not attend on a consistent basis. According to her file, she lived with her grandmother in Honduras and can read and write in her primary language, Spanish, at the third- and fourth-grade level. She is healthy, but her parents have indicated the transition at home, with Isabel trying to get used to living with them again, has been stressful. At the team meeting, Isabel's teachers appeared somewhat overwhelmed by her varied needs. Dr. Ketchum, the school psychologist, encouraged the team: "Each of these needs presents us—and Isabel—with a great opportunity!"

Reframing English Learners' Needs: From Challenge to Opportunity

English learners often appear to have multiple areas of need, sometimes including language acquisition, acculturation, and family separation. Some students, in addition, have backgrounds involved with poverty, trauma, or refugee experiences. While the instinct may be to look at these as negative factors requiring additional support and resources, it is essential to remember that these so-called negatives can provide great opportunities—opportunities for school personnel and opportunities for students themselves. Adopting such a viewpoint allows educators to support English learners by focusing on, and ultimately building, their strengths (Zacarian, Alvarez-Ortiz, & Haynes, 2017).

In this chapter, we discuss potential challenges facing English learners, underscoring the importance of shifting educators' mindsets to see these challenges as opportunities for growth and for building resilience. The introduction to this book mentions the growing concern with achievement and opportunity gaps for English learners. Such gaps can be exacerbated, or minimized, by how well school personnel are able to use multitiered systems of support, community school practices, and responsive decision-making. The use of inappropriate assessment and language support models also drives such gaps. This chapter will discuss some fundamental components and structures that must be in place to provide opportunities for students in an innovative and strengths-based framework, all of which subsequent chapters cover in more depth. However, we'll first look at some specific challenges that English learners may be likely to encounter.

English Learners and the Needs They May Bring to School

It bears repeating that educators cannot stereotype all English learners as having the same needs, nor can they ignore the assets and skills ELs have to see them only through a deficit lens. However, English learners are more likely to present with certain aspects of background and instructional needs (such as language learning needs). Additionally, other areas of need (such as exposure to trauma or refugee status) do not affect all English learners or even a majority of them, but they deserve attention from teams as they have potential to impact performance and functioning significantly. Descriptions of these follow.

Language acquisition. First and perhaps most obviously, English learners are in the process of English language acquisition. Some students come to school quite proficient in basic interpersonal communicative skills (BICS) but needing development in academic language (Cummins, 2008). Some come with strong native-language skills and a barely emerging English skill set. Most often, English learners are assessed on entry into a school system and assigned a stage or level of proficiency ("Level 1," "Level 2," and so on). Language acquisition needs may necessitate more processing time for English learners; it is reasonable to assume students will need explicit scaffolding and support for vocabulary, sentence structure and complexity, and pragmatic cues, to identify just a few areas (Freeman & Freeman, 2009; Pandey, 2012). For example, Kalu, age 9, arrived in school with strong literacy skills in his native language, Igbo. Having a naturally social personality, he quickly made friends and picked up day-to-day social language, which he further developed in frequent conversations with his friends about World Cup soccer and preferred video games.

Kalu's language and literacy skills in class, where all instruction occurs in English, were another story. He required far more processing time than his peers in reading, writing, listening, and speaking. Kalu's teachers noticed he was most successful when provided a list of core vocabulary in advance of each lesson and when sentence starters or paragraph frames supported his written and oral responses. Kalu also did well when paired with a peer buddy—particularly when his teacher reviewed expectations for productive behavior and provided visual signals and reminders for staying on task.

One recent change in terminology and mindset regarding English learners involves the idea of "emergent bilinguals." Rather than focusing on the extent to which English learners are limited in English skills, it may be useful to think of this population as "emerging bilinguals," emphasizing their strengths rather than the one thing they cannot do at the moment (speak English fluently). Furthermore, this view of English learners is helpful in establishing a linguistically responsive perception of students and may help team members to frame instruction as a process that builds off both language skill sets (García & Kleifgen, 2018). Let's look again to the example of Isabel, featured in the opening vignette, to illustrate this dynamic.

Isabel as an Emergent Bilingual

Mrs. Fitch, the reading specialist, was frustrated with Isabel's inability to make sense of the grade-level reading materials. "I know she's smart!" she exclaimed in the teacher's lounge. "I just don't know how to reach her with her limited English proficiency." Mr. Cardenas, the ESOL teacher, leaned over. "She doesn't just have limited English," he said. "Think of her as a bilingual learner, and maybe that will help you consider some other ways to reach her." Shifting her perspective a bit, Mrs. Fitch began to brainstorm ways to incorporate Isabel's native language into reading lessons. She finds Spanish texts and encourages Isabel to use those for oral reading and choice reading. She pairs her with Spanish-speaking peers and encourages native-language brainstorming. She makes sure to speak often in class about how students who grew up speaking another language should continue to use it, at home and at school. She encourages Isabel to complete reading response journals in Spanish until her English proficiency is more developed, and, as Isabel's English skills increase, Mrs. Fitch engages her in targeted discussions about similarities (and differences) between English and Spanish vocabulary, sentence structure, and language conventions. Using these strategies, she finds Isabel's engagement has improved, along with her reading skills.

Family separation. English learners, particularly those who are immigrants themselves or who have family members at various stages of the immigration process, are particularly at risk for family separation. Many English learners are living with extended family, are separated from parents temporarily or permanently, or are separated from other family members (Artico, 2003; Gill, 2006). Family separation can impact student performance and motivation in numerous ways. Students may be at increased risk for absences or tardiness depending on the availability of responsive adults. Students may also undergo affective changes as they experience separation, as separation can place students at risk for depression, withdrawal, or anxiety (Suárez-Orozco, Bang, & Kim, 2011). Extended absence may occur if students travel out of the country or across the state to visit family members. Students may also be at increased risk for poverty if separated from one or both parents. Finally, sudden changes in family status (deportation of a parent, for example) deserve special mention, as they can trigger abrupt declines in students' emotional well-being, school attendance, or academic performance (Giddling & Poggio, 2012).

Acculturation. Many students new to the United States, or to any cultural experience, face an acculturation process (Collier, 1998). This may, of course, include students born in the United States but new to school and American culture. The process of acculturation, or adapting to a new culture, typically includes a honeymoon or newcomer phase; a stage of gradual adjustment; a state of acculturation and adjusting expectations as well as behaviors; and, finally, attaining a level of comfort and mastery with the new culture. At any stage of the process, students may exhibit behaviors that differ from "typical" American classroom behaviors, both as a function of emotional upheaval and adjustment and as a function of cultural difference. The middle stages, involving gradual adjustment and adjustment of expectations, require particular care on the part of teachers, who may view atypical behaviors as symptomatic of disability or oppositional attitudes rather than, simply, cultural difference. One teacher of our acquaintance recounted the story of a kindergarten student who consistently did not meet expectations for respectful use of the bathroom. The student left toilet paper on floors, routinely did not flush, and allowed water to stream out of the sink and spill on the floor. In conversation with the student and in reviewing her file, the teacher realized this was the student's first experience with indoor plumbing; her "lack" of appropriate bathroom behaviors was, in fact, a function of a very different set of experiences. In fact, her behaviors were not inappropriate at all for her previous environment; she simply needed explicit guidance on how to use the bathroom in school.

Refugee experiences and trauma. English learners, particularly those who are refugees or recent arrivals, may have undergone trauma related to their journeys, experiences in their home countries, or their current living situations, any of which can impact well-being and functioning (Zacarian, 2015). Experiences such as wars, civil unrest, natural disasters, and famine, for example, can force children and families to seek new living situations repeatedly, and refugee camps, while they offer much-needed safety, may offer little in terms of educational programming (UNHCR, 2016). All of these experiences may cause trauma. The proportion of school-aged refugees is significant; in 2013, 34% of refugees were under 18 (National Academies of Science, 2017). In addition, English learners in the United States, like other children, are at risk for trauma associated with exposure to unsafe neighborhoods, violence, and other issues (Zacarian, Alvarez-Ortiz, & Haynes, 2017). All of these needs can result in a reduced ability to learn, underdeveloped self-regulation, and affective difficulty.

Legal status. As immigration policy continues to evolve, students and their families, particularly those who lack documentation, may experience transitions and stress due to changes in legal status. Even students who are citizens may be affected by the deportation, or potential deportation, of family members, as they may need to leave the country when their parents are deported or may experience significant disruption when parents are removed (National Academies of Science, Engineering, and Medicine, 2017). Legal status of parents or guardians may also affect families' eligibility for health care, social services and benefits, intensifying stress on students as well as their parents (Rice Doran, Mazur, & Llagas, 2012).

Poverty and related challenges. English learners are disproportionately likely to grow up in poverty, with nearly 35% in the bottom quintile, nationally, of household income, and fewer than 10% in the top quintile (National Academies of Science, Engineering, and Medicine, 2017). With poverty come other risk factors. The number of homeless English learners, for example, increased nearly 10% between the 2013–2014 school year and the 2014–2015 year, and ELs are the most numerous subgroup among homeless children generally (National Academies of Science, Engineering, and Medicine, 2017). Children in poverty, including English learners, are at increased risk for poor nutrition (Rice Doran, Mazur & Llagas, 2012) and chronic stress (Zacarian, Alvarez-Ortiz, & Haynes, 2017), which can cause physical and mental health difficulties and can affect students' abilities to learn.

Schoolwide Approaches to Support These Unique Needs

In the following chapters, some of these strategies and approaches will be discussed in more depth, including the ecological model and the use of response-to-intervention (RTI) and multitiered systems of support (MTSS), as well as family and community engagement. A brief overview of each of these follows here as an introduction.

Ecological model. English learners are often supported within isolated models using a deficit-based perspective (nonproficient English speaker) rather than a strengths-based view of English learners as emergent bilinguals. Indeed, research has increasingly focused on benefits of bilingualism in terms of neurological and cognitive development (Kovelmann, Baker, & Pettito, 2008). Looking at strengths

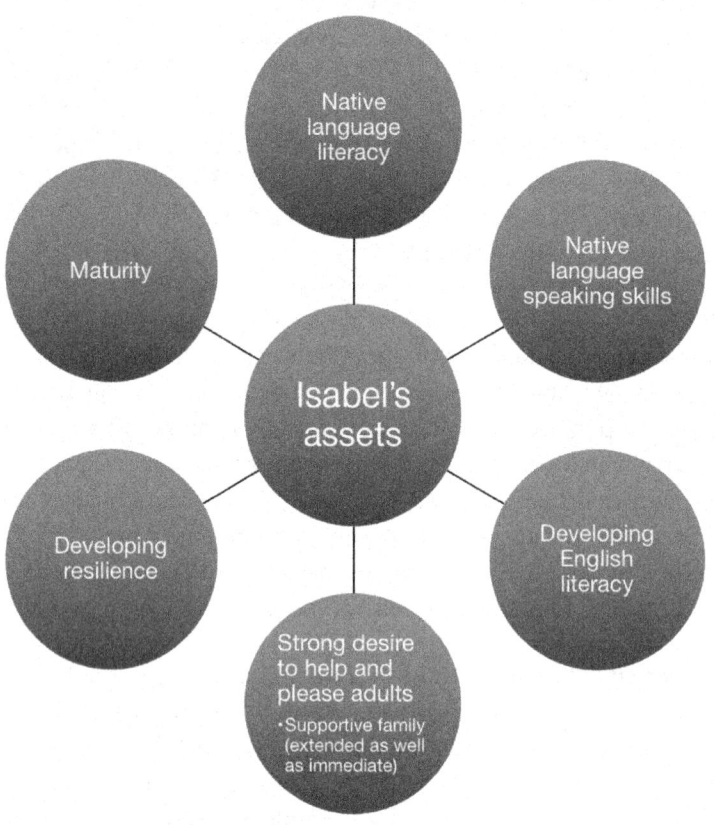

Figure 1: Sample asset map for Isabel

and benefits, as well as challenges, is part of the integrated approach suggested by ecological frameworks, popularized by Bronfenbrenner (1979). Variables to consider as a part of the student portfolio may include developmental needs, sense of belonging, cultural variables, and home language, along with basic needs. The case of Isabel represents a typical scenario in many schools.

In an ecological framework, it is helpful to assess variables intrinsic to a student as well as home, family, and community dynamics, to then develop effective supports. Teams may consider developing an asset map, where they can identify positive influences while also identifying challenges. Isabel's challenges may include possible trauma, interrupted instruction, resources, and recent family traditions, along with academic needs. To balance these challenges, Isabel also has native-language fluency and developing native-language literacy, opportunities to develop resilience, interest in pleasing adults, and developing English language skills. In her asset map, potential challenges are reenvisioned as strengths and used as starting points for Isabel's team to plan effective supports as well as enrichment when appropriate.

Effective problem-solving frameworks. By problem-solving frameworks, we mean schoolwide structures such as RTI, MTSS, or other consistently implemented approaches to collaboratively identifying and addressing student needs with fidelity. Unfortunately, while most schools have some version of student study or problem-solving, many such structures are not responsive to cultural and linguistic diversity and thus may perpetuate English learners' difficulties rather than address them (Orosco & Klingner, 2010). Appropriate use of RTI should involve teams considering culture, English language acquisition, and other factors unique to each student (Lopez & Mendoza, 2013). Implementing RTI can present significant challenges for school leaders, as well, such as the need for up-to-date staff development, new models of consultation, and consistent procedures for data-based decision-making (Meyer & Behar-Horenstein, 2015). Teams often work in isolation, and special education and general education often work in isolation from one another in schools with diverse learners (Meyer & Behar-Horenstein, 2015). In contrast, when RTI and multitiered systems are deployed appropriately, teams work together productively and communicate across grade levels, content areas, and disciplines.

Family and community engagement. Successful businesses know their clientele; successful schools and school systems know their families and communities and work closely with them. Research overwhelmingly shows that parent involvement leads to gains for both individual students and general family well-being. Student benefits include improved overall academic achievement, increased school attendance, fewer discipline problems, and greater educational aspirations (Epstein & Sanders, 2002; Hill et al., 2004; Nord & West, 2001). Family gains include improved parent self-confidence and overall family satisfaction with schools (Karther & Lowden, 1997). (See our website at www.tesol.org/exceptionalneeds for an overview of current legislation regarding family involvement and engagement.)

Although multiple strategies exist for fostering strong family and community partnerships, the evidence-based Community Schools Model will be discussed here, as it incorporates holistic integration of academics, health, and socioemotional variables in a paradigm responsive to families. The Coalition for Community Schools defines the community schools approach as a "place and set of partnerships between school and other community resources. Its integrated focus on academics, health and social services, youth and community development, and community engagement leads to improved student learning, stronger families, and healthier communities" (2013). Traditionally, services for physical and mental health are isolated from schools, but increasing research indicates benefits when mental health and physical wellness can be addressed within the parameters of the school community (Atkins et al., 2015; Klontz et al., 2015; Jimerson, Kilgus, & Reinke, 2015).

In one striking example of community–school partnership, Montgomery County Public Schools, outside the District of Columbia, has instituted community school collaborative partnerships in 29 schools, where the Montgomery County Department of Health and Human Services collaborates with the school system.

In a structure known as Linkages to Learning, each school is supported with an additional community school coordinator (CSC), family case manager, and child and family services personnel. Health-care services are provided on site in schools by a nurse practitioner, along with mental health personnel, and school-based social workers collaborate with families in problem-solving and mutual support, building trust among family members and professionals. This practice of creating trust-based relationships with parents and community is also foundational for implementation of a successful community school model (Khalifa, Arnold, & Newcomb, 2015). Seamless integration of services allows school personnel greater awareness of medical and psychological options to which they might direct parents; it allows students and parents to access needed services with minimal additional effort; and it allows health-care providers, including mental health providers, to see students and families in the school environment, an opportunity that may allow them to better appreciate specific needs and situations.

Moises: Trust-Based Relationships in Practice

Sensitivity to unique cultural perspectives and increased social cohesion are critical elements in trusting relationships (Khalifa et al., 2015; Blank et al., 2014). The team at Hillside Knolls Middle and High School works hard to cultivate trust-based relationships with all families, including those who are English learners. Moises is an EL in ninth grade who also has an IEP for a specific learning disability. His parents are very supportive but have limited time to support his learning, as each works two jobs. However, Moises's ESOL teacher and special education case manager are committed to a strong partnership with Moises's family. They call regularly to update his parents on his progress and send home information about small steps his parents can take to help him in his classes (reminding him to go to the library down the street, for example). Because Moises's mother does not have legal documentation, she is not comfortable attending meetings at the school during school hours, when she would be required to sign in and show an ID. Moises's caseworker routinely stays after school to hold meetings so that she can attend without needing to show ID (as district requirements for valid identification are less stringent when other children are not in the building). Moises's teachers have attended social functions at his house (his eighth-grade graduation party, for example) and even attended church with his family on important occasions (such as one day when Moises, who wants to be a minister, preached from the pulpit). Because of the investment of all parties—teachers and parents—and the mutual respect that exists among them, Moises knows he has strong support from all of the adults involved in his education. When questions or conflicts arise, such as discussions over length or type of services, the team is able to resolve them quickly because of this foundation of mutual regard.

Thinking about the impact of ecological approaches, effective problem-solving frameworks, and family and community engagement, let's consider how these issues play out in the case of Isabel, referenced at the beginning of this chapter. First, the team met before Isabel began to encounter academic or behavioral difficulty, knowing that she had needs that could present differently from the typical student's presentation. The school administrators made sure the team included the ESOL teacher, the special educator, the counselor, the social worker, the family liaison, and the literacy specialist, as well as the grade-level teacher. The team followed a protocol for discussing Isabel's needs, addressing strengths before discussing needs and ending with specific action steps. Finally, the family liaison, who had already met with Isabel's mother, concluded the meeting by offering to connect teachers with Isabel's family to continue constructive problem solving and support—for both Isabel and her family.

This list identifies variables the team should consider for Isabel (and similar students), beginning with language and addressing other aspects of her strengths and needs.

Language history (primary and secondary language—teams should assess speaking, listening, reading, and writing in both languages). Isabel's language assets should be considered early and positively. She has skills in Spanish (assessed at third- and fourth-grade levels) that make her an emergent bilingual. See www.tesol.org/exceptionalneeds for more information on the home language survey that schools administer to identify English learners.

Wellness, which includes social emotional wellness and overall health. Isabel's health appears stable, and the family has a positive report from her health-care provider. However, the school counselor routinely schedules a check-in with any student who has recently undergone transition in the home, and so Isabel will access this support.

Trauma. Because Isabel came from Honduras, an area highly affected by violence and children fleeing violence, the team should consider whether she has experienced violence or separation. If so, the team should consider what type of bilingual or cross-cultural counseling or emotional support services she may need, allowing her to express emotions and receive support in the language that best allows her to communicate.

Interrupted education, including exposure to prior learning and literacy opportunities as well as ESOL instruction. Many children who arrive from other countries, particularly those whose backgrounds may involve refugee experiences or whose families have sought asylum, undergo interrupted education. Maintaining schooling while completing multimonth, and sometimes multiyear, journeys to safety is challenging for families. In assessing her current levels of performance, Isabel's educators should consider her educational history and access to consistent schooling. Often, a focus on a child's educational history and prior learning opportunities can reinforce the strengths-based mindset discussed in this chapter; rather than seeing a child as "behind," reviewing a child's prior opportunities for learning can refocus team members on the learning that the student has managed to accomplish despite significant challenges.

Access to safe housing, adequate nutrition, and family support. In early conversations with Isabel's family, team members received the impression her family does have safe housing and is not currently experiencing food insecurity. However, Isabel will continue to need support related to trauma and her own transition between countries and environments. Additionally, she may need reinforcement and remediation in academic areas, along with a general orientation to "school culture" (when to pack up, what one does or doesn't take home each day, etc.). Most important, these services should be based in the awareness that Isabel has already demonstrated substantial resilience and adaptability by virtue of her experiences.

As teams consider these variables, which will occur in unique combinations for each student, they can use the Team Discussion Tool provided at www.tesol.org/exceptionalneeds to guide their discussions and planning. This tool spells out steps for teams to take in determining areas of strength and potential opportunities for support; it is designed to be used in the initial stages of intake and record review, though it can be utilized at any later point as well. The categories listed describe topics or areas to consider but are not presented as "negatives" or "positives"; rather, teams should review the existing data and consider how each unique student's experiences and strengths can be drawn upon in formulating interventions and supports to address any needs that may also exist.

As educators gain more information about students' areas of need as well as their strengths, this information can become the basis for collaborative planning to address those needs through well-designed instruction, targeted support, and intensive services when necessary. Coming chapters address these topics, but all of these approaches depend on accurate assessment of students' needs and understanding strengths-based approaches to supporting them.

Summary and Conclusion

Whatever challenges our English learners face, they can be seen rather as opportunities. They may include experiences with trauma or family separation; socioeconomic diversity; and language learning or educational needs. Fundamental student-centered processes and frameworks, including whole-child, ecologically based approaches (discussed more fully in chapter 4), collaborative problem solving (discussed more fully in chapter 5), and family and community engagement can provide educators with a valuable set of tools and resources to address English learners' needs.

Questions for Team Discussion or Shared Reflection

1. Does our school recognize the additional needs that our English learners may have? If so, do we reflect on those within the context of their overall strengths?
2. When considering English learners' needs, are we mindful of the different life experiences and stressors those students may bring with them?
3. Do we make conscious efforts to involve the families and communities of our English learners? If so, how do we do so? If not, what is one concrete improvement we can make in this area?

References

Artico, C. I. (2003). *Latino families broken by separation: The adolescent's perspective.* New York, NY: LFB Scholarly Publishing LLC.

Atkins, M., Shernoff, E., Frazier, S., Schoenwald, S., Capella, E., Marinez-Lora, A., . . . Bhaumik, D. (2015). Redesigning community mental health services for urban children: Supporting schooling to promote mental health. *Journal of Consulting and Clinical Psychology, 83*(5), 839–852. http://dx.doi.org/10.1037/a0039661

Blank, M., Mahaffey, R., & Villarreal, L. (2014). *Community schools are an essential equity strategy.* Retrieved from http://www.communityschools.org/assets/1/AssetManager/CS%20Equity%20Framework%20-%20Final%20Working%20Draft.pdf

Bronfenbrenner, U. (1979). *The ecology of human development: Experiments by nature and design.* Cambridge, MA: Harvard University Press.

Coalition for Community Schools. (2013). What is a community school? Retrieved from http://www.communityschools.org/aboutschools/what_is_a_community_school.aspx

Collier, C. (February 1998). Acculturation: Implications for instruction, assessment and intervention. Paper presented at National Association for Bilingual Education, Dallas, TX, 1998.

Cook, C., Frye, M., Slemrod, T., Lyon, A., Renshaw, T., & Zhang, Y. (2015). An integrated approach to universal prevention: Independent and combined effects of PBIS and SEL on mental health. *School Psychology Quarterly, 30*(2), 166–183. doi.org/10.1037/spg0000102

Cummins, J. (2008). BICS and CALP: Empirical and theoretical status of the distinction. In B. Street & N. H. Hornberger (Eds.), *Encyclopedia of language and education* (2nd ed., pp. 71–83). New York, NY: Springer.

Epstein, J. L., & Sanders, M. G. (2002). Family, school, and community partnerships. In M. H. Bornstein (Ed.), *Handbook of parenting: Vol. 5* (2nd ed., pp. 407–437). Mahwah, NJ: Erlbaum.

Freeman, Y., & Freeman, D. (2009). *Academic language for English language learners and struggling readers: How to help students succeed across content areas.* Portsmouth, NH: Heinemann.

García, O., & Kleifgen, J. (2018). *Educating emergent bilinguals: Policies, programs and practices for English learners* (2nd ed.). New York: Teachers College Press.

Gill, H. (2006). *Going to Carolina del Norte: Narrating the Mexican migrant experiences*. Chapel Hill, NC: The University Center for International Studies.

Gindling, T., & Poggio, S. (2009). Family separation and the educational success of immigrant children. (University of Maryland Policy Brief No. 7). Baltimore, MD: University of Maryland, Baltimore County.

Hill, N. E., Castellino, D. R., Lansford, J. E., Nowlin, P., Dodge, K. A., Bates, J. E., & Pettit, G. S. (2004). Parent academic involvement as related to school behavior, achievement, and aspirations: Demographic variations across adolescence. *Child Development, 75*(5), 1491–1509. doi:10.1111/j.1467-8624.2004.00753.x

Karther, D., & Lowden, F. (1997). The home-school contextual continuum of learning of families characterized as at-risk: Developmentally appropriate practice. *Journal of Early Education and Family Review, 5*, 8–13.

Khalifa, M., Arnold, N., & Newcomb, W. (2015). Understand and advocate for communities first: Efforts at education reform and other measures aiming to raise achievement levels will be more successful if schools first establish trust-based relationships with parents and their communities. *Phi Delta Kappan, 96*(7).

Klontz, B., Bivens, A., Michels, S., DeLeon, P., & Tom, L. (2015). The Mokihana Program: The effectiveness of an integrated department of education and department of health school-based behavioral health approach. *Psychological Services, 12*(2), 101–111.

Kovelman, L., Baker, S., & Petitto, L.-A. (2008). Bilingual and monolingual brains compared: A functional magnetic resonance imaging investigation of syntactic processing and a possible "neural signature" of bilingualism. *Journal of Cognitive Neuroscience, 20*(1), 153–169. https://doi.org/10.1162/jocn.2008.20011

Lopez, M., & Mendoza, M. (2013). We need to "catch them before they fall": Response to Intervention and elementary emergent bilinguals. *Multicultural Perspectives, 15*(4), 194–201. http://dx.doi.org/10.1080/15210960.2013.844604

Meyer, M., & Behar-Horenstein, L. (2015). When leadership matters: Perspectives from a teacher team implementing response to intervention. *Education & Treatment of Children, 38*(3), 383.

National Academies of Sciences, Engineering, and Medicine (2017). *Promoting the educational success of children and youth learning English: Promising futures*. Washington, DC: The National Academies Press. https://doi.org/10.17226/24677

Nord, C. W., & West, J. (2001). *Fathers' and mothers' involvement in their children's schools by family type and resident status* (NCES Publication No. 2001-032). Retrieved from https://nces.ed.gov/pubs2001/2001032.pdf

Orosco, M. J., & Klingner, J. (2010). One school's implementation of RTI with English language learners: "Referring into RTI." *Journal of Learning Disabilities, 43*(3), 269–288. doi:10.1177/0022219409355474

Pandey, A. (2012). *Language building blocks: Essential linguistics for early childhood educators*. New York, NY: Columbia Teachers' College Press.

Rice Doran, P., Mazur, A., & Llagas, C. (2012). Factors influencing needs of young dual-language learners and their families. (Young Exceptional Children Monograph Series 14: Supporting young children who are dual language learners with or at risk for disabilities). Arlington, VA: Council for Exceptional Children.

Suárez-Orozco, C., Bang, H., & Kim, H. (2011). I felt like my heart was staying behind: psychological implications of family separations & reunifications for immigrant youth. *Journal of Adolescent Research, 26*(2), 222–257. https://doi.org/10.1177/0743558410376830

UNHCR. (2016). *Missing out: Refugee education in crisis.* Retrieved from http://www.unhcr.org/57d9d01d0

Vaillancourt, K., & Amador, A. (2014). School-community alliances enhance mental health services: Resource-stretched schools can ensure comprehensive mental health care for students by creating partnerships with community-based service providers. *Phi Delta Kappan, 96*(4), 57–62. http://dx.doi.org/10.1177/0031721714561448

Zacarian, D. (2015). ELs living with trauma, violence and chronic stress. [Blog post]. Retrieved from http://blog.tesol.org/English learners-living-with-trauma-violence-and-chronic-stress

Zacarian, D., Alvarez-Ortiz, L. A., & Haynes, J.(2017). *Teaching to strengths: Supporting students living with trauma, violence, and chronic stress.* Alexandria, VA: ASCD.

Zayas, L. H. (2015). *Forgotten citizens: Deportation, children, and the making of American exiles and orphans.* New York, NY: Oxford

CHAPTER 3

A POLICY PRIMER

AMY K. NOGGLE AND GREGORY KNOLLMAN

Eterio's Pursuit of Education in the United States

The year is 1962. Eterio is a six-year-old boy who has just emigrated from Cuba with his grandmother and mother. Eterio's mother experienced complications during pregnancy. Eterio was born with a clubfoot and was delayed in many of his early milestones, such as sitting up, babbling, and learning to walk. Eterio's family was not able to locate appropriate educational services in Cuba, and with Castro's travel ban looming, they decided to leave the country to pursue the lauded educational opportunities in the United States. Upon arrival in the United States, they tried to register Eterio for a half-day kindergarten program at their neighborhood public school in Florida. Much to their dismay, they were told that there were no classes at the school for "kids like Eterio."

Historical Situation: Educational Rights for English Learners and Students with Disabilities

Historically, English learners and children with disabilities have been denied equal provisions in the public schools, and in some cases have even been mistreated. The road to ensuring an equal and meaningful education has been a tough one for both of these populations. Several key court cases, which will be described in the next section, play key roles in its history. Let's first revisit our country's political climate in the mid- twentieth century.

In the 1950s, the United States was experiencing a great deal of unrest regarding the inclusion of people from minority populations in all aspects of society. Tensions were particularly high surrounding the issue of equal access to education. Although African American students were entitled to a free education, their public school facilities were separate from those of white students. The United States was still operating under the outdated decision of the United States Supreme Court in the *Plessy v. Ferguson* case of 1896, the premise of which was the doctrine "separate but equal." The *Plessy v. Ferguson* decision upheld state-level segregation laws related to all public facilities including public schools.

Several federal policies impacting the rights to equal educational opportunities for individuals with disabilities and English learners connect to the civil rights initiatives and court cases in the 1950s and 1960s. Landmark decisions such as *Brown v. Board of Education* (1954) and changes in federal law with the passage of the Civil Rights Act of 1964 a decade later had a societal impact on the rights of minorities. Subsequent court cases including *Pennsylvania Association for Retarded Citizens (PARC) v. Commonwealth of Pennsylvania* (1972) and *Mills v. Board of Education of the District of Columbia* (1972) challenged state statutes and policies surrounding the education and equal participation of children with disabilities in public schools. Seminal cases such as *Lau v. Nichols* (1974) and *Casteñeda v. Pickard* (1981) established precedent for the treatment and provision of services to English learners. The civil rights legislation and court cases set the standard for the education of students with disabilities and English learners within the learning environment.

Brown v. Board of Education of Topeka (1954). Argued before the Supreme Court between 1952 and 1953 and then decided in May 1954, *Brown v. Board of Education* (1954) included a compilation of cases in which facts and conditions differed by geographic locale, but in all cases the plaintiffs argued that public schools segregated on the basis of race are not equal and cannot be made equal. These individuals were "deprived of equal protection of the law guaranteed by the Fourteenth Amendment." In seeking admission to nonsegregated public schools in their community, the opinion of the court delivered by Chief Justice Earl Warren noted that although prior cases dating back to *Plessy v. Ferguson* (1896) considered the doctrine of "separate but equal" public education had changed since the court's initial rulings.

In the opinion of the court, Warren noted, public education was viewed as an important function of state and local government, and compulsory attendance laws required that all youth of a certain age were to attend. The conditions of a segregated school denied children from minority backgrounds an equal education opportunity, not only due to the physical difference in certain school facilities and access to faculty and curriculum, but also due in large part to the greater impact that separation of children based on race has as a designation of inferiority between groups based on skin color. This sense of inferiority, the court also noted, could impact the motivation of children to learn and likely deprive them of the benefits they would receive in a racially integrated school system.

Brown v. Board of Education (1954) was viewed as a major underpinning for further civil rights action on behalf of other marginalized and disenfranchised groups (Yell, Rogers, & Rogers, 2012). Although it would take time for local systems to fully comply with the ruling, as a landmark civil rights case, *Brown v. Board of Education* (1954) forged a path for integrated and inclusive education for students of different races. During this turbulent but progressive time, other marginalized groups, such as students with disabilities and individuals from culturally and linguistically diverse backgrounds, gained a bit of inspiration and hope based on the *Brown* decision. Twenty years later, the Supreme Court would offer decisions on other cases involving the rights of these groups.

Court Cases that Forged a Path for Students with Disabilities

In the early 1950s, a parallel but related civil rights movement was brewing. Parental advocacy organizations such as United Cerebral Palsy (UCP) and the National Association for Retarded Citizens (NARC) were founded in an effort to secure rights and services for students with disabilities. By the early 1970s, these organizations had gained a great deal of momentum. In some cases, as you will see, state-based ARC chapters were prepared to take school systems to court.

> NARC has since changed its name to The Arc. This is due primarily to the fact that the term "retarded" is outdated and carries a certain negative connotation. The term was struck from references in federal law in 2017 and changed to "intellectual disabilities" (PL 111-256). The Arc is still an extremely active organization, with a state chapter in each of the 52 states and territories and over 700 regional chapters nationwide (The Arc, 2018).

Pennsylvania Association for Retarded Citizens (PARC) v. Commonwealth of Pennsylvania (1971). In Pennsylvania, PARC sued the commonwealth over a state law that required all children attain a "mental age" of five years prior to entering school. This antiquated law gave states the leverage to deny students a free public education. The judge in this case ruled that the existing statute was unconstitutional and subsequently declared that children with disabilities ages 6 through 21 must be provided a free public education and "training" regardless of ability level. Although this particular case was settled at the district level and never reached the Supreme Court, *PARC* certainly set a precedent and inspired other states to follow suit.

Mills v. Board of Education of District of Columbia (1972). Shortly after the *PARC* decision, friends and family of a young boy named Peter Mills sued the District of Columbia on behalf of Peter and seven other children. Peter was a 12-year-old boy who had been expelled from school due to behavioral issues; he was not allowed to return to school, nor was he afforded an alternate placement. The Board of Education of the District of Columbia alleged that Peter's education would be cost-prohibitive and burdensome. Sadly, the board had treated other children the same way. The judge in this case ruled in favor of the children; no longer could Peter's school discriminate based on disability, and ordered the school to create an educational program tailored to each child's needs. This case set the following precedents, which would ultimately appear in federal law: 1) Schools must provide accessible, free, and suitable education for all children of school age regardless of disability status, and 2) schools are not allowed to suspend a child for more than two days without a hearing.

Seminal cases such as *PARC v. Commonwealth of Pennsylvania* (1971) and *Mills v. Board of Education of DC* (1972) established protection for marginalized students with disabilities, just as *Brown v. Board of Education* (1954) had established protection under the Fourteenth Amendment for students from minority backgrounds (Yell, Rogers, & Rogers, 2012). As with the *Brown* decision, it would take time and additional federal legislation for states and local districts to comply with these court decisions. Students with disabilities continued to be denied appropriate public education, as local school systems argued insufficient funding, inadequate facilities, and limited instructional materials and training for teachers.

Court Cases that Paved the Way for English Learners

Individuals with disabilities and African Americans were not the only groups seeking protection from segregated school practices. Individuals from minority backgrounds including English language learners were also denied equal access and participation in public schools. Court decisions in the 1970s and 1980s established individual rights for English learners through the interpretation of newly enacted federal laws including Section 601 of the Civil Rights Act of 1964, the Bilingual Education Act of 1968 and 1974, and the Equal Educational Opportunity Act of 1974. (See Table 1 for a summary of educational laws and Table 2 for a summary of civil rights laws.) These laws established protection against discrimination on the basis of national origin and required those receiving federal funding and later all schools and districts to remove obstacles to equal participation for English learners. Landmark cases including *Lau v. Nichols* (1974), *Casteñeda v. Pickard* (1981), and *Plyler v. Doe* (1982) challenged public schools' treatment of English learners and established criteria for determining a school's compliance with the protections provided under the law. (Please note that *Diana v. California State Board of Education* (1970), one of the most critical court cases related to assessment of English learners, will be reviewed in chapter 8).

Table 1 **Summary of Educational Laws**

Year	Public Law Number	Title	Highlights of Resulting Legislation
1965	PL 89-10	Elementary Secondary Education Act (ESEA)	Title I: Provides educational assistance to schools serving low-income children; Title VII: First to recognize that ELs had specific educational needs (Title VII was merged with the Bilingual Education Act—see next section.) (Reauthorized as NCLB in 2001, and as ESSA in 2015; see below; also viewed as a civil rights law)
1968	PL 90-247	Bilingual Education Act	Provides state funds in the form of competitive grants to create programs for English learners, which includes teacher training, para-educator training, and parental involvement Does not require bilingual education but encourages schools to craft innovative means to teach English to nonnative speakers Initial focus was on low-income ELs; middle-class students with language barriers not included (Reauthorized in 1974, 1978, 1984, and 1988)
1975	PL 94-142	Education for All Handicapped Children Act (EHA)	Mandates a free and appropriate public education for all students, regardless of disability or perceived disability Establishes 11 different federally recognized educational disability categories Includes children ages 5 to 21 (Reauthorized in 1990, 1997, and 2004)
1986	PL 99-457	Amendments to EHA	Extends services for children with disabilities to preschoolers ages 3 to 5 Establishes incentives for states to start programs for infants and toddlers with disabilities (birth to 3)
1990	PL 101-476	Individuals with Disabilities Education Act (IDEA)	Reauthorized PL 94-142 and changed the name to IDEA Adds two new disability categories: Autism and Traumatic Brain Injury (TBI) Mandates transition services no later than age 16 Adds significant provisions for very young children (Part C) and students preparing to exit the special education system at 21

(continued on next page)

Table 1 (continued)

Year	Public Law Number	Title	Highlights of Resulting Legislation
1991	PL 102-119	Individuals with Disabilities Education Act Amendments	Developmental Delay (DD) added as a disability category, bringing the total to 14 Bolsters grant funding for college coursework related to the training of early interventionists
1997	PL 105-17	IDEA '97	Reauthorized IDEA Strengthens the least restrictive environment (LRE) mandate
2001	PL 107-110	No Child Left Behind (NCLB) Act	Reauthorized the ESEA of 1965 focusing on the following four components: results-based accountability, scientifically based curricula, greater parent involvement, and more control and flexibility at the local education agency (LEA) level
2004	PL 108-446	Individuals with Disabilities Education Improvement Act (IDEIA)	Establishes new requirements surrounding eligibility: • Specifies who can request an initial evaluation • Clarifies how states can determine whether a child has a specific learning disability (SLD) Allows districts to spend a greater percentage (up to 15%) of IDEA Part B funds on early intervening services**(EIS)
2015	PL 114-95	Every Student Succeeds Act (ESSA)	Reauthorized ESEA/NCLB Shifts accountability for English learners from Title III to Title 1 Changes term "limited English proficient" (LEP) to ELL or EL (See Table 4 for a comparison of NCLB and ESSA.)
2017	PL 111-256	Rosa's Law	Amends sections of the Rehabilitation Act of 1973, the Individuals with Disabilities Education Act (IDEA), and the Elementary and Secondary Education Act of 1965 (ESEA) by replacing the term "mental retardation" with "intellectual disability."

**Early intervening services (EIS) refers to response-to-intervention initiatives (RTI). EIS should not be confused with the more general term, "early intervention," which refers to services for infants and toddlers with disabilities, covered under Part C of IDEIA.

***Lau v. Nichols* (1974).** In the mid-1970s, non-English-speaking Chinese American students in San Francisco claimed they were being denied equal protection by the school system's failure to provide additional English language instruction. The Supreme Court ruled in favor of the students and did so by relying on Section 601

Table 2 **Summary of Civil Rights Laws**

Year	Public Law Number	Title	Highlights of Resulting Legislation
1964	PL 88-352 (78 Stat. 241)	Title VI of the Civil Rights Act	Prohibits discrimination in public accommodations, facilities, and schools, based on race, color, religion, sex, and national origin
1972	20 U.S.C. § 1681 et seq.	Title IX of the Educational Amendments	Prohibits discrimination against individuals on the basis of sex and exclusion from participation in federally funded education programs or activities in traditional educational institutions such as elementary and secondary schools, colleges or universities as well as education or training programs that receive federal financial assistance
1973	PL 93-112 (87 Stat. 394) 29 U.S.C. § 701 et seq.	Section 504 of Vocational Rehabilitation Act	Prohibits discrimination against individuals with disabilities in areas of education and employment by employers or organizations that receive federal funding (Amended in 1978 and 1984)
1974	20 U.S.C. § 1701	Equal Education Opportunities Act (EEOA)	Requires schools and districts to provide equal educational opportunity to all students regardless of race, color, sex, or national origin and prohibits denial of educational opportunity due to the failure of an agency to overcome barriers to a student's equal participation
1975	PL 94-142	Education for All Handicapped Children Act (EHA)	Mandates a free and appropriate public education for all students, regardless of disability or perceived disability (only serves ages 5 to 21) Also described as an educational law
1990	42 U.S.C. § 12101 et seq.	Americans with Disabilities Act (ADA)	Prohibits discrimination against individuals with disabilities in employment, education, and access to public accommodations

of the 1964 Civil Rights Act rather than on the Equal Protection Clause under the Fourteenth Amendment. Section 601 established protection against discrimination on the basis of national origin in federally funded programs.

While *Lau* did not mandate the use of a specific instructional approach to teaching, the case paved the way for future decisions regarding participation in educational programs for English learners (Hamayan, Marler, Sánchez-López, & Damico, 2013). Shortly after the *Lau* decision, the Bilingual Education Act of 1974 established a standard that states could not deny students equal opportunities based on race, sex, or national origin. Furthermore, educational agencies could not fail to take appropriate action to aid learners in overcoming language barriers that limit participation in educational programs.

Casteñeda v. Pickard (1981). Shifts in the research and political climate in the 1970s led to debate on the effectiveness of certain instructional approaches to teaching English learners. Researchers and practitioners in the 1970s and 1980s were interested in comparing students in bilingual and alternative English-only programs (National Academies of Sciences, Engineering and Medicine, 2017). Although prior law did not establish a specific instructional approach to teaching English learners, the decision rendered in *Casteñeda v. Pickard* (1981) by the Fifth Circuit Court of Appeals established criteria that districts must take into account to comply with the Equal Educational Opportunity Act of 1974.

Although this case did not make its way to the Supreme Court, and therefore the decision applies only to states within the jurisdiction of the Fifth Circuit, many courts across the country applied the criteria established in *Casteñeda* when determining a school's compliance with the Equal Educational Opportunity Act. Under the opinion of the court, schools must take appropriate action in basing their educational approach on sound theory, implementing it adequately, and evaluating it for effectiveness (Hamayan, Marler, Sánchez-López, & Damico, 2013).

Plyler v. Doe (1982). Shortly after the *Casteñeda* decision at the circuit level, a case also originating from the Fifth Circuit involving a Texas law that allowed the state to withhold school funds for undocumented children made its way to the Supreme Court. In this case, the Supreme Court ruled that states could not deny students a free public education based on their immigration status. The court found that this law violated the Fourteenth Amendment because it discriminated against students on the basis of a factor beyond their control and because this discrimination could not be found to serve a large enough state interest.

Federal Laws Related to English Learners and Students with Disabilities

The laws and landmark court cases enacted between the 1960s and 1980s set standards for students with disabilities and English learners. They emphasized the rights and equal protection of all learners regardless of race, sex, origin, ability level, or immigration status. Let's take a closer look at some of the important facets of key legislation related to English learners and students with disabilities, specifically Section 504 of the Vocational Rehabilitation Act, the Individuals with Disabilities Education Act of 1990, and the Every Student Succeeds Act (ESSA, 2015).

Section 504 of the Vocational Rehabilitation Act (1973). Many educators are familiar with the term "504 Plan," yet few may realize its longevity or origin. The Vocational Rehabilitation Act of 1973 is a civil rights law enacted to prevent discrimination against people with disabilities in all programs that receive federal funding. The most educationally relevant piece of this law is Section 504, which specifically addresses students with disabilities and ensures these students equal access and opportunity in the school setting. Section 504 provides guidance for an accompanying plan for educational accommodations, thus the term "504 Plan." This assurance is guaranteed for children in kindergarten through grade 12; although this is certainly an expansive age range, it is important to note that no provisions exist for infants, toddlers, or preschoolers with disabilities. Under Section 504, schools may be required to provide assistive technology, if deemed appropriate, to ensure that children with disabilities have equal access to an education. We will discuss assistive technology laws toward the end of this chapter, and we will present considerations and best practices in chapter 9.

By the early 1970s, the rights of people with disabilities had garnered national attention, and finally, it seemed that civil rights laws were answering the call to protect students with disabilities in the schools. However, Section 504 was not an educational law, and the civil rights law came with little guidance on eligibility definitions, procedural safeguards, and, perhaps most significantly, how individual states were to pay for specialized educations. By 1975, only 4 million of the 8 million children in our country with disabilities were receiving appropriate services (Pierangelo & Guilani, 2017). It was clear to many parents, lobbyists, and other activists that a comprehensive educational law for students with disabilities was long overdue.

Individuals with Disabilities Education Act (1990). The Education for All Handicapped Children Act (EHA, PL 94-142, 1975) was the first federal legislation to mandate a free appropriate public education for children with disabilities. In 1990, the law's name changed to the Individuals with Disabilities Education Act (IDEA). Over the past 40 years, the law and its subsequent amendments have either strengthened or expanded provisions to children and youth with disabilities by expanding access to early intervention services for infants and toddlers, emphasizing academic achievement and accountability, expanding development of transition planning for youth preparing for adulthood, and strengthening procedural safeguards to ensure parental input in the decision-making process.

The IDEA's most recent amendment, the Individuals with Disabilities Education Improvement Act (2004), is arranged into several parts. Title I justifies the law and defines terms; it includes information regarding the state grant programs, educational requirements for students ages 3 to 21, discretionary support for infants and toddlers, discretionary support for state personnel development, technical assistance to states, model demonstrations, personnel preparation, and support programs such as the establishment of parent training and information centers, among others. Title II of the amendments in 2004 established the National Center on Special Education Research within the Institute of Education Sciences. The center sponsors research and evaluates the effective implementation of the IDEA (Yell, 2012).

There are many important components of the IDEA (Smith, Tyler, & Skow, 2018; Yell, 2012). Although the law is not specifically limited to a few key provisions, we will highlight several of its aspects, including the right to a free, appropriate education; the delivery of service in the least restrictive environment; access to appropriate evaluations; involvement of parents and students in the decision-making process; the development of individualized education programs; and the provision of procedural safeguards to protect students and inform parents of their rights under the law. A description of each of these components follows.

Free appropriate public education (FAPE). The IDEA guarantees the right to services for all children with identified disabilities who are eligible for special education services, regardless of their ability level, at no additional cost to the parents. (We present a full list of categorical disability definitions under the IDEA in chapter 8). The state and local education agencies also have a responsibility to identify students struggling to make progress in school, and, if appropriate, to offer evaluations in areas where delays are suspected, to determine if eligibility for special education services is appropriate.

Least restrictive environment. Schools must provide access to a variety of educational placement options for students with disabilities. Access to general education should be considered in addition to the appropriate accommodations, modifications, and supplementary aids and services required to meet the needs of learners with identified disabilities. Schools are required to consider a child's neighborhood school (sometimes referred to as the "home school" or "catchment area school") prior to considering other, more restrictive options.

Appropriate evaluation/nondiscriminatory and multidisciplinary assessment. An evaluator trained in areas where a child has a suspected disability must conduct the evaluation. The evaluation is used to help determine the child's eligibility for special education services as well as to identify areas to emphasize in meeting the child's needs. As you may imagine, assessments can present a number of challenges, especially when the aspects of disability and language barrier are combined. Chapter 8 covers this process at length, providing operational definitions for both "nondiscriminatory" and "multidisciplinary" and offering guidance regarding specific assessment tools.

Individualized education program (IEP). The IEP is a written statement or document developed by a team of people, often as part of an annual meeting, to determine educational services for students with identified disabilities and for whom special educational services are recommended. Chapter 10 includes an in-depth discussion of considerations for developing IEPs for English learners. An IEP meeting can comprise a broad and often diverse group of people including, but not limited to, parents, teachers, administrators, an educational psychologist, and the student. The IEP includes, but is not limited to, a statement on the child's present level of academic achievement and functional performance (PLAAFP) as well as current evaluation results. Team members use this information to help them make an informed decision about the program. Some of the components of an IEP document might include the setting in which the child will receive educational services, the accommodations or modifications that might be necessary to help the child within the general education curriculum, the special education and related services to be provided, and the educational goals that will best meet the needs of the child within their educational program.

Procedural safeguards. Schools are required to inform parents of their rights along with notifications and prior written consent regarding issues related to identification, evaluations, and eligibility for and placement in special education services. Parents are permitted to request an independent evaluation, review all educational records, and follow procedures to request access to mediation or a due process hearing. Schools are also required to present materials to parents in their primary language and must provide access to interpreters, when requested by families, for the purposes of educational meetings.

Parent and student involvement in decision-making. Parents and students are encouraged to be active and equal participants in the decision-making process involving their applicable special education programs. Parents also have a right to participate in all meetings, provide or withhold consent for evaluations, and make informed decisions. Students are also encouraged to remain informed about the decisions made pertaining to the services and supports they will receive as part of their individualized education programs. They are encouraged to attend meetings when appropriate and, once reaching an age when needs surrounding their transition from school are discussed, they should be present as active members of the decision-making team.

Section 504 v. IDEA. Many parallels exist between these two landmark laws, but they are notably different from one another. For example, not all children with disabilities will necessary qualify for special education services under the IDEA; however, a child with what may be perceived as a mild or a hidden disability will qualify for accommodations under Section 504. "Hidden" disabilities include those not easily observed, such as asthma, epilepsy, attention deficit disorder (ADD), and allergies (US Department of Education, 2015). Table 3 presents a side-by-side comparison of Section 504 and the IDEA.

No Child Left Behind Act. In 2001, the No Child Left Behind Act (NCLB) ushered in a shift in accountability for our educational system. This law mandated the use of scientifically proven educational strategies and interventions, as well as statewide testing for students in the K–12 system, regardless of disability, native language, or immigration status. Although certain exceptions could be made for students with disabilities (see Table 4), NCLB required annual state testing in reading and math for all students in grades 3 through 8 and once in high school; children in grade spans 3 through 5, 6 through 8, and 10 through 12 were to be tested in science content as well. With this new high-stakes testing came a great deal of apprehension among public school administrators and teachers, which likely stemmed from the "adequate yearly progress," or AYP, requirement. Each local school district was

Table 3 **A Comparison of Section 504 and IDEA**

Section 504	IDEA
Section 504 of the Vocational Rehabilitation Act of 1973	Originally passed as the Education for All Handicapped Children Act (EHA) in 1975
Civil Rights Law	Educational Law
Protects "school-age" children only (K–12)	Originally mandated services for children ages 5 to 21; current law covers children from birth to age 21
Substantive standard is "equivalency"	Substantive standard is "educational benefit"
Not federally funded	Federally funded
Accompanying educational document includes accommodations: **504 Plan**	Accompanying educational document for children ages 3 to 21 includes accommodations among **many other** sections: Individualized Education Plan (IEP)
	Accompanying intervention document for children ages birth to 3 is the Individualized Family Service Plan (IFSP)
Enforced by the Office of Civil Rights (OCR)	Enforced by the Office of Special Education Programs (OSEP)

required to show that its students were making AYP based on pre- and posttest scores on these state assessments. Although NCLB certainly included children with disabilities and English learners in the scope of its data capture, advocates for these groups of students were concerned that the tests would not be meaningful for them, nor would students be likely able to show the AYP as mandated by this law.

Every Student Succeeds Act. The Every Student Succeeds Act (ESSA, 2015) is the most current version of the original Elementary Secondary Education Act (ESEA) passed in 1965. The ESEA, viewed by some as both a civil rights and an educational law, was the first to recognize that English learners have specific educational needs. Title VII of the ESEA captured these needs, and this section was eventually merged with the Bilingual Education Act. Title I of the ESEA also provided educational assistance to schools serving low-income children. The needs of low-income children, ELs, and children with disabilities have certainly persisted over time and in many cases intersect. With the wheels set in motion by the ESEA (1965), Section 504 (1973), and EHA/IDEA (1975), public schools worked hard in the latter half of the twentieth century to provide equitable and meaningful opportunities for these vulnerable populations of students. Despite these efforts, many achievement gaps persisted. Legislators and policy makers believed that it was time for an overhaul of the ESEA.

In 2015, the Every Student Succeeds Act (ESSA) replaced NCLB. With the passage of ESSA came revised requirements and a certain degree of clarification regarding the inclusion of English learners and students with disabilities. These revisions are presented in Table 4.

Table 4 **Side-by-Side Comparison of NCLB and ESSA**

Criteria	**No Child Left Behind (NCLB, 2002)**	**Every Student Succeeds (ESSA, 2015)**
English learners (ELs): accountability and definitions	Requires districts to annually assess all students with limited English language proficiency (LEP)	Shifts accountability for English language learners into Title I; allows schools to phase in the use of English language learners' test results for accountability purposes Replaces term "LEP" with "ELL" or "EL"
	Required that 100% of students be proficient in reading and math by the end of school year 2013–14. Requires that schools make adequate yearly progress (AYP) for all students and for subgroups for which data are disaggregated	Eliminated AYP and the 100% proficiency requirement Requires state-developed accountability systems for all English language learners: English language proficiency to be measured annually in grades 3–8 and once in high school
	Establishes student subgroups for accountability and data disaggregation, including students who are economically disadvantaged, have limited English language proficiency (LEP), have disabilities, and belong to major racial and ethnic groups as determined by the state	Establishes three new subgroups for data reporting only: homeless status, students with parents in the military, and students in foster care All other original subgroups remain the same.
Students with disabilities: accountability and definitions	Requires states to apply the same academic standards to all schools and children	Allows states to develop alternate academic achievement standards for students with the most significant cognitive disabilities using a documented and validated standards-setting process
	Requires states to provide reasonable adaptations and accommodations for students with disabilities Allows states to administer alternate tests to students with disabilities; however, these alternate tests could be administered to no more than 1% of the total number of students being assessed.	Requires states to provide reasonable accommodations for students with disabilities Allows states to administer alternate tests for students with *the most significant cognitive* disabilities; however, these alternate tests may be given to no more than 1% of the total number of students being assessed.

Summary and Conclusion

Let's revisit the story of Eterio from the beginning of the chapter with current legislation in mind.

Eterio's Pursuit of Education in the United States

The year is 2019. Eterio is a six-year-old boy who has just emigrated from Cuba with his grandmother and mother. Eterio's mother experienced complications during pregnancy. Eterio was born with a clubfoot and was delayed in many of his early milestones, such as sitting up, babbling, and learning to walk. With Castro's travel ban recently lifted, they decided to leave the country to pursue the lauded educational opportunities in the United States.

Upon arrival in Florida in August, his mother tries to register Eterio for a half-day kindergarten program at their public neighborhood school. She learns that it is a "Title I" school, though she is not sure what that means. Much to her liking, she is told that Eterio is old enough to be considered a first-grader and will therefore be entitled to a full-day of school. (The state of Florida still does not require full-day kindergarten.) The school secretary locates the school's Spanish-speaking liaison (covered under Title 1 funds of ESSA) and sends her out to help Eterio's mother fill out the necessary registration records. Through the liaison, the family learns that the school has ESOL services. The liaison also notifies the grade 1 instructional team leader (ITL), the ESOL team leader, and the building special educator. Although the special educator was testing another child when Eterio's mother first visited, she asks a translator to bring them in for a face-to-face meeting. Eterio's mother doesn't believe she is allowed to bring her own mother with her to the meeting. The school team tells her that she may bring anyone she likes for support. The family brings all of their medical records to the meeting, and they are told that Eterio may qualify for specialized services under IDEIA (2004). However, it is first necessary for the team to decide which tests will be done and by whom (multidisciplinary assessment) and to obtain his mother's permission to test him (procedural safeguards). His mother worries that Eterio will not be able to start school until after the testing is completed, but the school team assures her that he can start with the other students on the first day of school. He will be pulled from his first-grade classroom periodically during the assessment process. His mother is told that all assessments will be completed within 60 days, which is an IDEIA (2004) requirement. (Note: We present timelines for the assessment process in chapter 8.)

This scenario paints a much happier picture for Eterio compared to his situation in 1962. Over the past several decades, our county has seen a huge shift in the rights, both educational and civil, for English learners and students with disabilities. No longer are students turned away because they don't "look" like other students; no longer can schools segregate students based on race, ability/disability, or language barrier; and no longer are schools allowed to deny students individualized educational services due to purported lack of funding or staffing. In this chapter, we have summarized key legislation through the lens of both populations and have attempted to highlight the overlap and convergence of such laws. When the worlds of disability and language barriers intersect, as in the case of Eterio, it is critical to understand the nuances of all laws that protect English learners with disabilities.

Questions for Team Discussion or Shared Reflection

1. Consider both the initial and concluding vignettes about Eterio's journey. Which components of the IDEA come into play in the concluding scenario to ensure that Eterio receives adequate services? Identify at least 3 components and explain how they protect Eterio and support his learning needs.

2. How did the *Brown v. Board of Education* (1954) decision pave the way for students with disabilities and students who are culturally and linguistically diverse (CLD)?

3. After reviewing Table 1 summarizing some of the federal educational laws, what are the three most recent disability categories added to the IDEA? Are you surprised that these categories were not added earlier?

4. How does ESSA reflect a more "modern" view of English learners? Who is Rosa? What impact did she have on the labels of our current disability categories under the IDEA? Is there any other terminology in our current school culture that you would consider outdated?

References

Americans with Disabilities Act of 1990, 42 U.S.C. § 12101 *et seq.*

Brown v. Board of Education, 347 U.S. 483 (1954).

Casteñeda v. Pickard, 648 F 2d 989 (5th Cir. 1981).

Civil Rights Act of 1964, 42 U.S.C. § 2000d.

Education Act Amendments of 1972, 20 U.S.C. § 1681 *et seq.*

Education Act Amendments of 1974, PL No. 93-380, 88 Stat. 580.

Education Act Amendments of 1990, 20 U.S.C. § 1401 *et seq.*

Education for All Handicapped Children Act of 1975, 20 U.S.C. § 1401 *et seq.*

Hamayan, E., Marler, B. Sánchez-López, C., & Damico, J. (2013) *Special education considerations for English language learners: Delivering a continuum of services* (2nd ed.). Philadelphia: Caslon Publishing.

Individuals with Disabilities Education Act. (1990). In *IDEA: Individuals with Disabilities Education Act.* Retrieved from https://sites.ed.gov/idea

Individuals with Disabilities Education Act Amendments of 1997, 20 U.S.C. § 1401 *et seq.*

Individuals with Disabilities Education Improvement Act of 2004.

Lau v. Nichols, 441 U.S. 563 (1974).

Mills v. Board of Education of the District of Columbia, 348 F. Supp. 866 (D.D.C. 1972).

National Academies of Sciences, Engineering, and Medicine. (2017). *Promoting the educational success of children and youth learning English: Promising futures.* Washington, DC: The National Academies Press. Retrieved from https://www.nap.edu/catalog/24677/promoting-the-educational-success-of-children-and-youth-learning-english

Non-regulatory guidance: English learners and Title III of the Elementary and Secondary Education Act (ESEA), as amended by the Every Student Succeeds Act (ESSA). (2016). Retrieved from https://www2.ed.gov/policy/elsec/leg/essa/essatitleiiiguidenglishlearners92016.pdf

Pennsylvania Association of Retarded Citizens (PARC) v. Commonwealth of Pennsylvania, 334 F. Supp. 279 (E.D. Pa. 1972).

Pierangelo, R., & Giuliani, G. A. (2017). *Assessment in special education: A practical approach.* (4th ed.). Boston, MA: Pearson.

Plessy v. Ferguson, 163 U.S. 537 (1896).

Plyler v. Doe, 457 U.S. 202 (1982).

Rehabilitation Act of 1973, Section 504, 29 U.S.C. § 794 *et seq.*

Smith, D. D., Tyler, N. C., & Skow, K. G. (2018). *Introduction to contemporary special education: New horizons.* (2nd ed.). New York, NY: Pearson.

The Arc: Who we are. (2018). Retrieved from http://www.thearc.org/who-we-are

US Department of Education. (2015). *The civil rights of students with hidden disabilities under Section 504 of the Rehabilitation Act of 1973.* Retrieved from https://www2.ed.gov/about/offices/list/ocr/docs/hq5269.html

Yell, M. L. (2012). The Individuals with Disabilities Education Act. In M. L. Yell (Ed.). *The law and special education* (3rd ed.). (pp. 63–92). Boston, MA: Pearson.

Yell, M. L., Rogers, D., & Rogers, E. L. (2012). The history of the law and children with disabilities. In M. L Yell (Ed.). *The law and special education* (3rd ed.). (pp. 45–62). Boston, MA: Pearson.

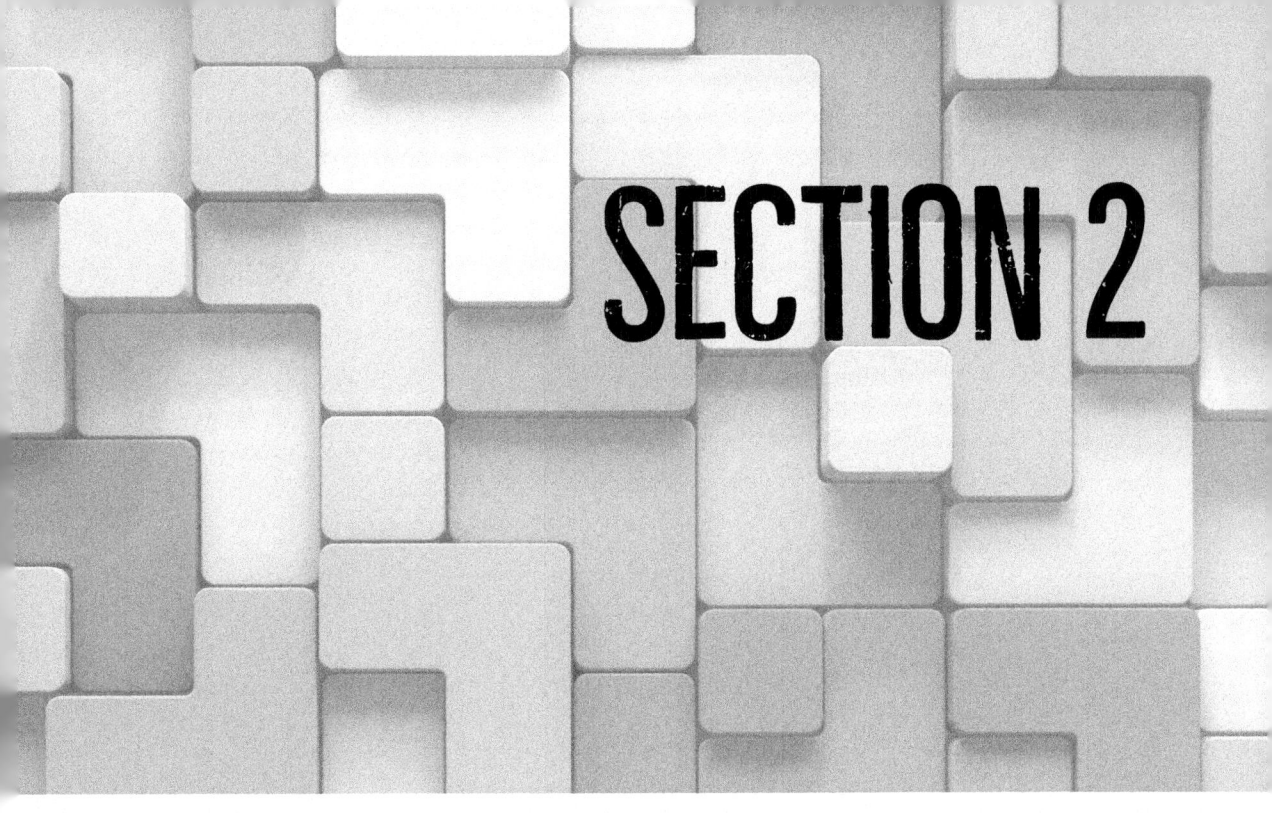

SECTION 2

CLASSROOM STRUCTURES

CHAPTER 4

ECOLOGICAL APPROACHES AND MULTITIERED SYSTEMS OF SUPPORT: HOLISTIC APPROACHES TO SERVING ENGLISH LEARNERS

PATRICIA RICE DORAN AND DANIELLE TURNER

Continuous Improvement at Ellen Ochoa Elementary School

Over the years, teachers at Ellen Ochoa Elementary School have worked consistently to improve their practice. Ellen Ochoa has seen its English learner enrollment rise from 14% in 2012 to 46% in 2017. Of that 46%, half receive ESOL services and another quarter have recently exited from ESOL. Additionally, Ellen Ochoa has seen its culturally and linguistically diverse (CLD) population grow consistently, with numerous ethnicities and nationalities represented, for a total of 60% ESOL enrollment. Most recently, the community has experienced a large influx of families from Haiti and from Senegal, further diversifying the school population. As the proportion of English learners increases, teachers have found ways to ensure they are meeting all students' needs. Continuous, and sometimes critical, self-assessment is part of that process.

It is often easiest to visualize specific concepts and paradigms when authentic examples are provided. The school described here is a composite based on several schools we have worked in or collaborated with. Throughout this chapter, key concepts from the literature will be illustrated through anecdotes about the process of continuous improvement and responsive decision-making undertaken by the staff at Ellen Ochoa Elementary, as well as selected other vignettes related to individual students.

A robust multitiered system of supports (MTSS) framework incorporates developmentally and culturally appropriate expectations at all stages of instruction and intervention (Esparza Brown, & Doolittle, 2008; Hamayan, Marler, Sanchez-Lopez & Damico, 2013). In any system that provides appropriate services and supports to English learners with disabilities, early intervention and strong collaborative practices are essential. This chapter provides an overview of MTSS frameworks, which allow teams to collaborate early in the intervention process to ensure students are receiving linguistically appropriate instruction, reducing the likelihood of inappropriate referrals. The use of MTSS processes can also ensure that, if and when students move to eligibility determination for special education, adequate documentation exists that culturally and linguistically appropriate instruction, assessment, and intervention have already been tried. Therefore, the use of collaborative, student-focused, multidisciplinary procedures constitutes an essential—if early—part of the special education journey for English learners who may have disabilities.

Increasingly, researchers understand that learning is a dynamic process in which students interact with many factors in their environment (Normak, Pata, & Kaipainen, 2012). An ecological approach sees students as being dynamically connected to their environment and leverages their unique assets for instruction and socioemotional development (Esparza Brown & Doolittle, 2008; ASCD, n.d.). First developed by Urie Bronfenbrenner (1977), ecological systems theory posits that each individual exists within a larger set of systems within their environment. An individual, in fact, cannot be understood apart from their environment, as the different systems within one's environment continuously affect, and are affected by, the individual. Bronfenbrenner continued to adjust this model, most recently proposing a bioecological model (Bronfenbrenner & Ceci, 1994; Bronfenbrenner & Morris, 2007) that integrates new scientific knowledge of genetic, biological, and environmental influences on growth and development. Ecological models are useful for conceptualizing the relationships among students, schools, and cultures, as a responsive and open understanding of students' cultural backgrounds is essential for creating a well-functioning school system (LaSalle, Meyers, Varjas, & Roach, 2015). An ecological approach also fits well with the use of tiered intervention processes, which incorporate a continuum of systems and supports through all aspects of the instructional process and all intensities of student needs (Esparza Brown & Doolittle, 2008).

RTI, MTSS, and Whole-Child Approaches

In recent years, many schools have shifted from a response-to-intervention (RTI) paradigm to an MTSS structure. The RTI paradigm, which came into widespread popularity after the Individuals with Disabilities Education Improvement Act (IDEIA, 2004) (Fuchs & Fuchs, 2006), requires schools to provide high-quality general instruction to all learners (often referred to as Tier 1), to use universal screening to identify students who may be at risk, to provide targeted supports and interventions to those learners (Tier 2), and to monitor progress using appropriate data to provide more intensive interventions (Tier 3) to those who are not successful, or do not "respond" to Tier 2 supports (RTI Action Network, n.d.; Echevarria, Richards-Tutor, & Vogt, 2015). Like RTI, MTSS models incorporate high-quality universal instruction, data-based decision-making, and increasing intensity of supports, often referred to as "tiered instruction" or "intervention." In addition, MTSS models often emphasize systemwide approaches to problems, collaboration, and holistic decision-making about students (Sink, 2016; Reschly & Cooloong-Chan, 2016), which make these models a particularly good fit with ecological approaches to student support and success. Tiered interventions should, in fact, integrate knowledge of language, culture, development, and other variables best considered within an ecological framework (Esparza Brown & Doolittle, 2008). When implemented effectively, RTI or MTSS approaches take into account a variety of sources of information about any given student, including academic performance, language proficiency, cultural background, family status, socioemotional well-being, socioeconomic status and needs, and other relevant data. This way of looking at students, emphasizing all aspects of their well-being and functioning, is often referred to as the "whole-child approach" or, more broadly, the "whole school, whole community, whole child (WSCC) model" (ASCD, n.d.).

The WSCC model, developed by ASCD, a leading curriculum and administration organization, is an "ecological approach" that features "the school . . . drawing its resources and influences from the whole community and serving to address the needs of the whole child" (ASCD, n.d.). In a whole-school, whole-community, whole-child paradigm, all parties collaborate to bring about the best outcomes for students, conceived broadly in terms of physical, mental, socioemotional, and academic well-being. School counselors, nurses, social workers, and cafeteria staff might all play important roles in supporting students and implementing evidence-based practices. Collaboration among schools, community partners, health agencies, and social services personnel is an essential element of the model as well. The Centers for Disease Control (CDC, n.d.) has recently embraced this model as a means of promoting better health and positive outcomes among school-aged children, their families, and their communities. The WSCC model, and its predecessor, the whole-child approach, are particularly appropriate for meeting the needs of English learners, who may arrive at school with numerous assets as well as numerous areas where they will benefit from understanding and appropriate supports, including legal, socioemotional, nutritional, and cultural/linguistic ones (Rice Doran, Mazur, & Llagas, 2012). Please see www.tesol.org/exceptionalneeds for an example of how the staff at Ellen Ochoa drew on concepts from the WSCC framework to support one particular student.

Metrics for student well-being in the WSCC framework. On its Whole Child Initiative website (http://www.ascd.org/whole-child.aspx), ASCD provides state and national "snapshots" of data, which present key metrics regarding children's academic, social, and physical well-being. For 2015, national data indicated that only 54% of children had home access to amenities such as libraries and parks (ASCD, 2015). Only 68% of children had had preventative-care medical checkups in the preceding year, and 20% reported being bullied at school in the preceding year (ASCD, 2015). For states, districts, and schools, identifying similar metrics relevant to students' well-being, and tracking them over time, may provide insight into the types of support students, families, and communities have and the types of supports they may need.

Schools often track academic and behavioral data, such as quarter grades, benchmark assessments, attendance, suspensions, and office referrals. In addition, schools can track less traditionally discussed variables to provide additional perspectives. These may include community or individual indicators of health and social and socioeconomic well-being; utilization of counseling or health-care services; and student and family interactions with faculty or staff. In his film *Who Cares About Kelsey?*, Dan Habib chronicles one low-performing school that asked faculty to record their positive interactions with students to identify which students had had none. These students were then targeted for positive interaction and encouragement (Habib, 2012). The following indicators may provide schools and teams some additional metrics to review in tracking the well-being of the "whole school."

- **Family engagement:** Report cards returned within a given timeframe; families attending social events or parent workshops; families completing students' weekly literacy logs; family responses to phone, email, or social media surveys administered in multiple languages

- **Student health and well-being:** Student nurse or health center visits; student counselor or social worker visits; teacher referrals to counselor; students reporting hunger; students requesting additional breakfast or lunch; parent/family use of school social or behavioral services; parent/family use of school-based health services or referrals; students receiving medication at school; students complying with medication regimen at school

- **Student academic risk/growth:** Family rating scales administered in multiple ways and multiple languages; students' running records for reading; students' growth in ESOL; bilingual progress monitoring data; students' project grades; students' rubric-based grades; students self-report using rating scales; rate of students exiting ESOL.

Key Elements of Schools Built for Diverse Learners

Based on our own experience and current research, we can identify several elements that are particularly important for schools implementing an ecological, whole-school/whole-community/whole-child approach. These are described here, with specific examples from Ellen Ochoa Elementary to illustrate essential points.

Culturally sustaining focus. In recent years, researchers have pioneered the concept of "culturally sustaining pedagogies," an updated approach to culturally responsive practices (Paris, 2012; Paris & Alim, 2017). Rather than simply appreciating, accommodating, or supporting students' cultures, sustaining pedagogy focuses on actively encouraging, building, and institutionalizing students' minority cultures (Paris, 2012). Schools with a culturally sustaining focus actively affirm students' identities, languages, and cultural backgrounds. In practice, this means a school's cultural outreach goes beyond the typical food night or cultural diversity week; it also means that schools work with families at all stages of the educational process, seeking and utilizing family input on cultural appropriateness of curriculum, instruction and school policies and procedures.

Ensuring All Cultures and Families Are Included

The teachers at Ellen Ochoa spend the first three weeks of school learning about their students' backgrounds. Students share explicitly about their home cultures and traditions, and—equally important—share one-on-one feedback with teachers about how they like to learn, what their prior experiences of school are, and how they want their teachers to relate to them. At the beginning of the year, teachers review the state curriculum standards and district curriculum documents and discuss how those documents fit into their students' and families' backgrounds and belief systems. Teachers actively seek textbooks and classroom library materials that represent children of all ethnicities. They plan strategies and activities with an eye toward accommodating children from collectivist, rather than competitive, cultures. Students are encouraged to code-switch in class and to write in their native languages. Bridging cultures, biculturalism, and resilience are frequently incorporated into lesson topics in subjects ranging from math and humanities to PE. Thanks to the school's family liaison, all class websites and letters home to parents are translated into Spanish, and the family liaison recently reached out to a local university for assistance in translating information into other languages as well. Family nights at school are alternated with school nights out in the community, where teachers and administrators gather at popular restaurants, church halls, or other venues to meet with parents and family members.

Explicit privileging of family and community. While all, or nearly all, schools acknowledge the importance of family involvement, schools often pursue policies and approaches that limit spheres of family involvement or constrain families' abilities to influence decision-making. These limitations run counter to the ecological framework, where families and communities are understood to be foundational in students' growth and development (McDonald, Miller, & Sandler, 2015). At some schools, for example, families are encouraged to participate in Parent-Teacher Association (PTA) meetings, but are not invited to curriculum committee meetings, the assumption being that parents are effective in supporting the work of schools, but teachers, and schools, are the real experts on learning and retain power in the relationship (Hong, 2011). In responsive and culturally sustaining schools, by contrast, family involvement is constant and meaningful. Parents may be asked to provide input on school and district curriculum decisions, advise on school policies or intervention protocols, and participate on interview and hiring committees. Similarly, the community as a whole is viewed as a source of strength and resources for all members of the school community (Verdon, Wong, & McLeod, 2016). Culturally sustaining schools often have strong relationships with community members, including pastors, organizers, and extended families (Ross, n.d.). Particularly for schools with large numbers of English learners, staff must realize that family and community involvement may take a different shape than they expected and may also evolve over time as families become more engaged in the school community (Baird, 2015).

Meaningful Relationships with Families

Over the last two years, the administration of Ellen Ochoa Elementary has encouraged teachers to cultivate meaningful relationships with parents. To that end, the school hosts parent feedback nights, where parents provide open feedback to administrators about what they feel is and is not working. Parents sit on the school's curriculum and instruction committee, and a parent representative sat on the committee that interviewed assistant principal candidates the previous spring. Parents and community members provide input on relevance and effectiveness of lessons and materials through a variety of mechanisms, including email, focus group meetings, and parent feedback nights along with committee participation. When a student needs additional support, parents are contacted before any interventions are provided, so that parent awareness and collaboration are already present should the team move forward to more intensive supports.

Consideration of developmental norms. In an ecological framework, schools acknowledge that students develop at unique and individual rates and that students' growth cannot be considered apart from their environments. Expectations for academics and behavior are developmentally and culturally appropriate, and student needs in these areas are also addressed as part of a developmental process. Any considerations for student intervention, support, or services should occur as part of a broader examination of student development. The checklist provided in Figure 1 provides an example of how a school might apply these developmental norms to student intervention and support; student chronological age is considered as a potential factor influencing classroom performance.

Another important element of a developmental focus is a "growth mindset" (Dweck, 2009; Dweck, 2015), which reframes failures or shortcomings as opportunities for growth and development.

Considering Development and Potential for Growth

In monthly team meetings for student interventions, teachers at Ellen Ochoa begin by discussing factors such as a student's chronological age in relation to grade-level peers, acculturation processes, and recent family needs or stressors. "Problems" are reframed as areas where students are still developing skills, and the language the team uses has been changed to reflect this growth-based, developmental focus (teachers frequently add the word "yet," to statements of challenges: "He does not turn in homework" becomes "He has not yet consistently turned in homework"). Rather than focusing on how far below grade level a student is, teachers select one skill and provide the student targeted support in developing it. Of course, the ESOL teacher is part of all of these discussions to ensure that academic expectations are appropriate to the student's language development as well as physical, social, and emotional growth. (See www.tesol.org/exceptionalneeds for a sample discussion guide teams can use to guide these conversations.)

Student's name: _____

Strengths: _____

Birthday: _____ Does the child's behavior coincide with age? Is s/he older/younger than others?

Guardian(s): _____

Contact with guardian(s)/dates: _____

Street address: _____

Attended kindergarten at _____

ESOL Level: 1   2   3   4   5   REL   N/A

Family Concerns   Attendance Issues   Social Challenges
     Y/N   Y/N   Y/N

Social Services Client   Medical Concerns   Behavior Concerns
     Y/N   Y/N   Y/N

Admin Consulted   Counselor Consulted   Cumulative Folder Consult
     Y/N   Y/N   Y/N

Further information for all categories marked Yes:

Math: Above/Below/On Level (Based on current work and/or past report card)

   Benchmark Scores

Reading: Above/Below/On Level (Based on current work and/or past report card)

   Benchmark Scores

Top two concerns regarding student and strategies implemented to address them:

1. _____

2. _____

Two questions you want answered in the problem-solving meeting (i.e., strategy ideas, timeline for process, group advice for supporting child/family)

1. _____

2. _____

Figure 1: Data recording form for team review and consideration (Credit: Jessica Blasic. Used with permission.)

Positive school climate. School climate should be positive for all learners, including all ethnic, cultural, regional, or language groups (Gonzales, Eades, & Supple, 2014; LaSalle, Meyers, Varjas, & Roach, 2015). In practice, this may mean providing unique ways of demonstrating that staff care about students (García et al., 2013) and nurturing them all. Mentoring, teacher-student support networks, use of the native language, and affinity groups can all help to support students from minority cultural or language backgrounds. School climate has been demonstrated to exert a positive or a negative impact on student achievement and language outcomes (Brown, 2015). For these reasons, a positive climate, including positive approaches to school discipline, is essential in any culturally sustaining framework.

Intentional Affirmation of Students

Teachers at Ellen Ochoa go out of their way to affirm all students. Each week, a student of the week is selected from each classroom, with selection criteria honoring growth, tenacity, or grit, and kindness to others along with more traditional measures of academic achievement. A council of fourth- and fifth-grade students provides input to the leadership team about how students are feeling, a practice that is particularly useful when controversial issues come up in the national or local news or when potentially disruptive events occur in the community. Teachers have recently begun instituting elements of restorative justice, encouraging students to consider how their actions impact others rather than simply punishing inappropriate behavior and moving on. Each week, the principal and assistant principal stop by at least half of the classrooms in the school to praise students for what they are doing well. When students seem to experience difficulty, they are quickly paired with an adult mentor in the school who checks in on them regularly and provides them encouragement and positive feedback—while also screening to ensure more targeted supports are not needed. The school once utilized an incentive system for positive behavior but has moved on from that in favor of providing authentic praise and positive adult attention to each student.

Interprofessional and interdisciplinary collaboration. The WSCC model requires collaboration not only among educators but between educators and noneducators (ASCD, n.d.). Providing holistic, multidimensional support to English learners may require assistance from health-care professionals, counselors, community members, and other agency representatives such as social workers, hospital staff, and juvenile or adult justice system representatives. Schools with strong interdisciplinary, ecological structures develop networks of partners who can support students, families, and teachers. They will also establish times and processes for communication among all of these various professionals.

Collaboration to Support All Students

Student support team meetings at Ellen Ochoa routinely include the school nurse, the school psychologist, and the school counselor. Representatives from special education, such as speech, occupational therapy, and physical therapy professionals, attend on a rotating basis. The assistant principal serves as the liaison for the district's integrated health-care and mental health programs, and she invites health-care and mental health workers to most meetings. If their schedule does not permit them to attend, she follows up with them weekly about specific students. Teams have also developed procedures to facilitate review of data across disciplines; it is not uncommon for classroom teachers to share behavioral data with counselors or mental health professionals, and, where parents consent, medical professionals share health data with teachers. As a result of proactive outreach to parents, and careful explanations of how student privacy would be protected, increasing numbers of parents have agreed to allow professionals to share information. In one meeting in February, teachers changed their approach to Veronica's behavior when they learned that her entire family had had the flu for the past week and that Veronica was being treated for a resistant sinus infection that followed her bout with flu. Teachers determined that they would wait to assign homework until she recovered so that she could focus on rest and recovery; they were careful to use redirection and positive encouragement, recognizing that unfocused or inattentive behavior may be a result of discomfort or illness rather than choice. Last, they identified a time in Veronica's schedule each day when she can check in with the school nurse, who coordinates referrals to her primary care practitioner.

Strengths-based approach. As described in chapter 1, English learners are well served by a strengths-based approach that emphasizes their gifts and leverages the assets in their families and communities to provide needed resources and support.

Involving the Family Liaison

At Ellen Ochoa Elementary, the school's family liaison is part of problem-solving meetings, where she can contribute valuable information about context and community. Discussions of each individual student begin with identifying what that student does well and how they contribute to the classroom. On more than one occasion, thoughtful consideration of these strengths ("Nicholas is very eager to help") has helped teams to realize that the behavioral deficits they had identified ("He often interrupts peers and insists on being called on before other students") could become assets with some positive encouragement and occasional redirection ("I'll remind him that other students get turns to be classroom helpers as well, and we can identify some special jobs that can be assigned just to him.").

Additional Considerations for Implementing Ecological Approaches in Schools

A few additional considerations are relevant for schools seeking to implement, or strengthen, an ecological approach to student support. These include careful reflection on the ESOL teacher's role and constant consideration of how developmental norms are taken into account. A brief discussion of each follows.

The ESOL teacher's role in an ecological framework. Being an ESOL teacher may feel overwhelming at times, particularly in schools where ecological perspectives on student well-being are emphasized. Suddenly, in addition to being the expert on students' language acquisition, the ESOL teacher may feel expected to speak with authority on culture and acculturation, family circumstances, community dynamics, and even health or mental health issues. Holistic and ecological perspectives, however, should not be interpreted to place undue burdens on ESOL personnel or any other staff. Rather, ESOL teachers provide a unique perspective on students' language and acculturation, and they frequently—but not always—can serve as connections between families and schools or communities and schools. Other personnel can likewise provide support to ESOL teachers; counselors can ensure their services are available to all students equally, regardless of language or background, so that English learners, as well as other students, can address any affective needs that might otherwise interfere with learning.

Chapter 5 explores the specific parameters of the ESOL teacher's role in responsive problem solving for English learners who may have disabilities. In the brief discussion here, we will note that school leaders can also provide support for the ESOL teacher in accomplishing this unique role by modeling openness to input from ESOL staff, consulting ESOL teachers on a regular basis, and ensuring that teaching schedules provide adequate time for ESOL personnel to be part of problem solving and consultative groups. In addition, school leaders can ensure that ESOL teachers are not required to carry the responsibility of serving English learners in isolation. Some practical ways to accomplish this include making expectations clear for all staff regarding linguistically appropriate instruction; providing frequent professional development opportunities for staff on second-language acquisition, ESOL curriculum, and linguistic accessibility; and providing sufficient support services for diverse learners, including those learning English and their families within the building, so that ESOL and other teachers can refer students and families as needed.

Reference to cultural as well as medical and social norms for development. Many accepted norms for child development are, in fact, culturally bound (Rubin & Menzer, 2010); US (and many Western) teachers may expect school-aged children to be relatively independent and assertive, while such behavior would be considered developmentally inappropriate in Eastern societies (Rubin & Menzer, 2010). Harry and Kalyanpur (2012) speak of "redefining" the "parameters of normalcy" (p. 12) to ensure that school-based expectations for developmental milestones, delays, and disability truly reflect student needs as opposed to cultural bias. Behavioral concerns based on cultural constructs such as self-care, socially appropriate behavior, socialization and collaboration, personality, and industriousness should certainly be carefully scrutinized for cultural bias before school personnel assume a student has a developmental need, or requires intervention, in any of those areas. See Table 2 for a partial list of developmental skills that may be culturally or linguistically bound.

Table 2 Skills and Attributes that Culture or Language May Influence

Language:	receptive skills (listening and reading)
Language:	expressive skills (speaking and writing)
Language:	nonverbal communication skills (nodding, body language, eye contact)
Language:	pragmatics and understanding of social cues (including patterns of initiating or participating in conversations)
Personal:	self-care (dressing, self-feeding, etc.)
Personal:	independence and comfort separating from parent/family
Personal:	norms for hygiene and personal care (including use of restrooms, cleaning products, etc.)
Academic:	study skills and group work skills (including comfort level with group and partner work, particularly when groupings are diverse in terms of language, gender, or culture)

Summary and Conclusion

Given the rich and complex backgrounds of many English learners, an ecological, tiered framework offers school personnel the opportunity to provide support in a variety of areas, communicating and coordinating among personnel from many disciplines while also considering the strengths and needs of the student as well as their school, family, and community. Integrating whole-child perspectives requires team members to consider data from multiple sources, to evaluate their own awareness of cultural and developmental norms, and to collaborate with personnel who may not be in their day-to-day group of colleagues.

Questions for Team Discussion or Shared Reflection

1. How has our school integrated ecological perspectives into our planning, our instruction, and our academic or behavioral interventions?
2. Do we currently coordinate information, supports, and services from personnel with health, mental health, community, language, and academic expertise? If not, would it be useful to do so, and how can we begin?
3. Do we have mechanisms in place to ensure that the needs we identify are not simply a function of culture? In other words, how are we ensuring that we are not identifying students for intervention who simply have a different cultural perspective related to communication, social interaction, or school activities?
4. Do we have mechanisms in place to ensure that the interventions we propose are responsive to the student's background, level of development, and family status?

References

Association for Supervision and Curriculum Development. (n.d.). Learning and health: Whole school, whole community, whole child. Retrieved from http://www.ascd.org/programs/learning-and-health/wscc-model.aspx

Association for Supervision and Curriculum Development. (n.d.). *Whole school whole community whole child: A collaborative approach to learning and health.* Alexandria, VA: ASCD:

Association for Supervision and Curriculum Development. (2015). Whole child snapshot: United States. Retrieved from http://www.ascd.org/ASCD/pdf/siteASCD/wholechild/snapshot/2015/2015-us-ascd-whole-child-snapshot.pdf

Baird, A. S. (2015). Beyond the greatest hits: A counterstory of English learner parent involvement. *The School Community Journal, 25*(2), 153–175.

Bronfenbrenner, U. (1977). Toward an experimental ecology of human development. *American Psychologist, 32*(7), 513–531. http://dx.doi.org/10.1037/0003-066X.32.7.513

Bronfenbrenner, U., & Ceci, S. J. (1994). Nature-nurture reconceptualized in developmental perspective: A bioecological model. *Psychological Review, 101*(4), 568–586. doi:10.1037/0033-295X.101.4.568

Bronfenbrenner, U., & Morris, P. A. (2007). *The bioecological model of human development.* In R. M. Lerner & W. Damon (Eds.), *Handbook of child psychology: Theoretical models of human development* (pp. 793–828). Hoboken, NJ: John Wiley & Sons Inc. doi.org/10.1002/9780470147658.chpsy0114

Brown, C. (2015). *The educational, psychological, and social impact of discrimination on the immigrant child.* Washington, DC: Migration Policy Institute.

Centers for Disease Control. (n.d.). WSCC Fact Sheet. Retrieved from https://www.cdc.gov/healthy youth/wscc/pdf/wscc_fact_sheet_508c.pdf

Cummins, J. (2001). *Negotiating identities: Education for empowerment in a diverse society.* (2nd ed.). Los Angeles, CA: California Association for Bilingual Education.

Dweck, C. (2009). *Mindset: The new psychology of success.* New York, NY: Random House.

Dweck, C. (2015). Carol Dweck revisits the growth mindset. *Education Week, 35*(5), 20, 24.

Echevarria, J., Richards-Tutor, C., & Vogt, M. E. (2015). *RTI and English learners: Using the SIOP model.* Upper Saddle River, NJ: Pearson.

Esparza Brown, J., & Doolittle, J. (2008). A cultural, linguistic, and ecological framework for response to intervention with English language learners. *Teaching Exceptional Children, 40*(5), 66–72.

Fuchs, D., & Fuchs, L. S. (2006). Introduction to response to intervention: What, why, and how valid is it? *Reading Research Quarterly, 41*(1), 93–99. doi:10.1598/RRQ.41.1.4

García, O., Woodley, H., Flores, N., & Chu, H. (2013). Latino emergent bilingual youth in high schools: Transcaring strategies for academic success. *Urban Education, 48*(6), 798–827. https://doi.org/10.1177/0042085912462708

Gonzalez, L. M., Eades, M. P., & Supple, A. J. (2014). School community engaging with immigrant youth: Incorporating personal/social development and ethnic identity development. *School Community Journal, 24*(1), 99–117.

Habib, D. (2012). *Who cares about Kelsey?* Durham, NH: DH Photography and University of New Hampshire Institute on Disability.

Hamayan, E., Marler, B., Sanchez-Lopez, C., & Damico, J. (2013). *Special education considerations for English language learners: Delivering a continuum of services* (2nd ed.). Philadelphia: Caslon.

Harry, B., & Kalyanpur, M. (2012). *Cultural reciprocity in special education: Building family-professional relationships.* Baltimore, MD: Brookes Publishing.

Hong, S. (2011). *A cord of three strands: A new approach to parent engagement in schools.* Boston: Harvard Educational Publishing Group.

Individuals with Disabilities Education Improvement Act of 2004.

LaSalle, T., Meyers, J., Varjas, K., & Roach, A. (2015). A cultural-ecological model of school climate. *International Journal of School & Educational Psychology, 3*(3), 157–166.

McDonald, L., Miller, H., & Sandler, J. (2015). A social ecological, relationship-based strategy for parent involvement: Families and Schools Together (FAST). *Journal of Children's Services, 10*(3), 218–230. doi.org/10.1108/JCS-07-2015-0025

Normak, P., Pata, K., & Kaipainen, M. (2012). An ecological approach to learning dynamics. *Educational Technology & Society, 15*(3), 262–274.

Paris, D. (2012). Culturally sustaining pedagogy: A needed change in stance, terminology, and practice. *Educational Researcher, 41*(3), 93–97.

Paris, D., & Alim, H. S. (2017). *Culturally sustaining pedagogies: Teaching and learning for justice in a changing world.* New York, NY: Teachers' College Press.

Reschly, A. L., & Cooloong-Chan, M. (2016). Contextual influences and response to intervention. In S. R. Jimerson, M. K. Burns, & A. M. VanDerHeyden (Eds.), *Handbook of response to intervention: The science and practice of multi-tiered systems of support* (2nd ed., pp. 441–453). New York, NY: Springer.

Rice Doran, P., Mazur, A., & Llagas, C. (2012). Factors influencing needs of young dual-language learners and their families. (Young Exceptional Children Monograph Series 14: Supporting Young Children who are Dual Language Learners with or at Risk for Disabilities). Arlington, VA: Council for Exceptional Children.

Ross, G. (n.d.). *The community is McNabb Elementary.* Retrieved from https://www.pbis.org/common/cms/files/pbisresources/201_08_03_McNabbPBIS.pdf

RTI Action Network. (n.d.). What is RTI? Retrieved from http://www.rtinetwork.org/learn/what/whatisrti

Rubin, K., & Menzer, M. (2010). Culture and social development. *Encyclopedia of Early Childhood Development.* Retrieved from http://www.child-encyclopedia.com/sites/default/files/textes-experts/en/601/culture-and-social-development.pdf

Sink, C. (2016). Incorporating a multi-tiered system of supports into school counselor preparation. *The Professional Counselor, 6*(3), 203–219. doi:10.15241/cs.6.3.203

Verdon, S., Wong, S., & McLeod, S. (2016). Shared knowledge and mutual respect: Enhancing culturally competent practice through collaboration with families and communities. *Child Language Teaching & Therapy, 32*(2), 205–221.

CHAPTER 5

COLLABORATIVE PROBLEM SOLVING FOR ENGLISH LEARNERS: THE UNIQUE ROLE OF THE ESOL TEACHER

HEATHER WAYSON WILSON

Collaborative Problem Solving in Action with Josefina

At age 5, Josefina starts kindergarten. Only 3 days before, Josefina had entered the United States. Shortly after the first marking period, her teacher refers Josefina to the problem-solving team for possible special education screening. The teacher identifies an urgent need for intervention because "she can't even identify the first letter of her name, 'J.'" The classroom teacher is also concerned about short-term memory and retention of information.

The ESOL teacher is a core member of the problem-solving team. He informs the team that the letter "J" in English sounds very different from the letter "J" in Spanish. (In Spanish, "J" is not pronounced as it is in "jump," but rather as it sounds in "Jose.") The ESOL teacher also shares information on Josefina's level of performance and progress. He notes Josefina's strengths in responding well to songs and dancing, in her eagerness to write, and in knowing to start sentences with a capital letter and end with a period. He relays that while Josefina's ESOL Level 1 in reading and speaking are low, she is an English Level 4 (out of 5) in listening, and that perhaps not knowing enough English vocabulary is depressing some of her performance data particularly as they relate to retention. He notes that Josefina does not speak voluntarily in conversational dialogue. Even in a small-group setting, he notes Josefina is very hesitant and shy, and she seems to lack confidence. The team agrees Josefina will continue to receive support from her ESOL teacher, and they will monitor her progress, not moving forward to screening. Josefina is assigned a fifth-grade peer buddy.

By the spring of kindergarten, Josefina can count to 20 and, having entered without being able to identify any letters, can identify 25 of 26 letters. Her teachers note the peer buddy seems to have helped her confidence. Josefina displays more willingness to take risks and to engage in conversation in the classroom. Josefina also enrolled in an extended learning opportunity with the homework club.

In this vignette, Josefina's performance improved, in large part, because the collaborative problem-solving process at her school worked as it was designed to work. While teachers felt comfortable raising concerns, team members, such as the ESOL teacher, were able to use their own specialized knowledge to offer further information, provide insight on potential causes for student difficulties, and brainstorm alternative approaches to support the student. In this chapter, we build on the overview of responsive problem solving provided in chapter 4 and explore in greater depth the role of ESOL personnel in facilitating this process. In particular, we will review elements of the problem-solving process, particularly those most conducive to successful planning for English learners with and without disabilities.

Collaborative problem-solving processes may work differently in each district and school, although careful planning should always be part of the process (RTI Action Network, n.d.). For example, some school processes might rely on monthly cross-grade-level meetings; others might utilize weekly grade-level meetings. In some schools, related-services providers (speech and language therapists, occupational therapists, counselors, and physical therapists) might attend all team meetings, while others may involve classroom teachers as core members and related-services professionals on an as-needed basis. However, all successful teams are likely to have certain features in common. One essential element is the substantive involvement of the ESOL teacher as a core member of the problem-solving team (Ferlis & Yaoying, 2016; Peercy, Dotter, & DiStefano, 2017). The ESOL teacher can be an effective advocate for appropriate decision-making and can educate team members about second-language acquisition and its impact on learning. In particular, the ESOL teacher can play several important roles, which include supporting the work of teams at meetings, educating colleagues about second-language acquisition, and informing them about EL-friendly classroom environments and instruction.

ESOL Teacher Impact at Team Meetings

In schools serving many diverse learners, the ESOL teacher should be an integral part of problem-solving and team meetings and can play several important roles in collaboration and in student-focused discussion (Martin-Beltran & Peercy, 2014; Ferlis & Yaoying, 2016). Listed here are a few particularly appropriate considerations for ESOL teachers to address.

Strengths-based solutions. Until the ESOL teacher highlighted Josefina's strengths, the staff member was actively discussing identification of the student for special education services. Once the ESOL teacher communicated that the sound for the letter "J" is different in English than in Spanish, Josefina's native language, the teacher and team could begin to understand that the underlying reason for the behavior might be due to second-language acquisition and not a necessarily a learning difficulty. The ESOL teacher was also able to relay strengths to the team, including that Josefina's listening comprehension in her native language was considerably higher than other areas such as speaking or reading. Furthermore, the ESOL teacher noted that, while Josefina was shy and hesitant to speak in small-group settings, she responded well to songs and dancing, was eager to write, and knew to start sentences with capital letters and end with periods. Rather than invoking intensive intervention or special education services, the team implemented more support from the ESOL teacher for Josefina, and assigned her a fifth-grade peer as a buddy to become more engaged in groups.

Language accessibility. Not only were language-related and other supports provided for Josefina, the school developed a structure in which the ESOL teacher could offer support for the team of teachers. The teachers did not understand the language demands of the curriculum. Josefina's name begins with "J." They were concerned she could not identify "J." Yet, "J" is pronounced differently in English than in Spanish. The ESOL teacher collaborated with the team to specify the expressive skills needed to reach the content objective.

Universal Design for Learning. The integration of Universal Design for Learning (UDL) (Ralabate & Lord Nelson, 2017) will be discussed at length in chapter 6. However, any introduction to problem solving must touch on the importance of UDL in identifying appropriate solutions for English learners experiencing difficulty in the classroom. In fact, selecting and implementing targeted interventions is inappropriate if the student has not yet had access to high-quality, universally designed instruction (Ralabate & Lord Nelson, 2017); problem solving at the early stages should instead focus on ensuring the student receives UDL-based instruction. Drawing on his own familiarity with UDL, the ESOL teacher was able to further underscore the need for the specific teacher to implement the UDL principles of multiple means of engagement, representation, and action and expression. See our website www.tesol.org/exceptionalneeds for a list of specific ways the ESOL teacher encouraged the team to integrate UDL for Josefina.

Native-language integration. The ESOL teacher used Josefina's native language to validate the difficulty she was having in English. In this case, by providing data on how Josefina was performing, listening, speaking, reading, and writing in her native language, the ESOL teacher was able to invalidate the teacher's information that Josefina was not making sufficient progress.

School staff often describe concerns about an English learner as they would learning difficulties a student with special education needs would experience. Such descriptions may arise from an inadequate understanding of the difference between the two groups of students, an area of ongoing challenge for schools and school systems (Klingner & Eppolito, 2014). In this case, because Josefina could not identify first letter of her name, the teacher assumed Josefina was exhibiting the behavior of a student with learning disabilities. With the EL expert on the problem-solving team, the team was able explain why Josefina was not learning and begin to design appropriate interventions and support based on a valid explanation of her needs. Guided by the ESOL teacher, the team began by assuming the English learner was a student with typical development experiencing language-related challenges, rather than assuming the presence of a disability. Working from this assumption, the team began to address the process of determining interventions from an English learner's perspective rather than from a disability perspective.

Educating Team Members About Second Language Development

The ESOL teacher collaborated with the team in developing the intervention and supports Josefina needed. His expertise in second-language learning was critical in problem solving for this student. While Josefina at first appeared to be making minimal progress, she ended the year having made steady progress.

As the expert on English learners and second-language development, the ESOL teacher plays a key role in helping team members understand the second-language acquisition process and other elements unique to supporting English learners (Martin-Beltran & Peercy, 2014). In particular, the ESOL teacher is uniquely positioned to help teachers and team members

- Know and understand the language development of the student in their native language/s;
- Assess and plan for effective communication in the native language/s and create opportunities to build communication skills;
- Leverage the home language through instructional materials, activities, and assessments as appropriate;
- Understand and interpret the student's educational history, including learning experiences in native language/s and in English;
- Determine whether difficulties in English language use also appear to exist in the native language/s (this may, of course, require specialized assessment and interpretation). (To get this information, the staffs need to collaborate with the ESOL teacher to see if the student is developing typically.)

Supporting the Classroom Environment and Instruction

Last, any problem-solving effort must ensure that students have received appropriate instruction prior to referral. Some English learners are taught in "disabling contexts," with too few opportunities to receive appropriate instruction matched to their needs and too few opportunities to develop their oral language and literacy skills (Klingner & Eppolito, 2014). The ESOL teacher, over time, can work with team members to consider the degree to which their classroom environments are truly accessible. On a related note, ESOL teachers can also play an important role in helping staff understand what a comprehensible classroom might look and sound like. For example, what types of support, instructional strategies, or scaffolding could be used to help English learners access and engage with the content through language? Providing such support can free up cognitive space for learning content so that students are able to focus on the substantive learning at hand.

ESOL teachers' roles may or may not take them into general education, content classrooms. When in classrooms, ESOL teachers may be occupied by delivering their own curricula, either through coteaching with a general education colleague or in a parallel small-group lesson. Therefore, the time for collaborative consultation may be minimal, despite the fact that this type of informal, one-on-one, or small-group planning is among the most widely endorsed models for coteaching and collaboration (Friend & Cook, 2017). ESOL teachers may have the greatest influence, not in the classroom, but in daily or weekly discussions with colleagues. These may occur informally, in the hallway or teachers' lounge, as well as formally at team meetings and student support discussions.

In such settings, some effective questions can help to open space for all participants to consider how accessible their instruction and curricula might be for English learners. ESOL teachers might consider asking one or more of these questions when a colleague describes difficulty reaching an English learner:

- Are you sure the student understands basic classroom routines and procedures?
- Is the curriculum accessible to the student? Is the language of the textbook, workbooks, and assessments consistent with the student's ESOL level?
- Are you adjusting expectations for written work, or reading performance, in accord with the student's ESOL level?
- Is the student in the process of adjusting to a new culture, new country, or new school? If so, are you or others providing any kind of support to the student to assist with this process?

ESOL teachers can play a crucial role in helping students use oral and written language within a meaningful context. They can, furthermore, encourage colleagues to connect instruction to students' cultures, backgrounds, and experiences (Ortiz et al., 2011). They can help colleagues to model language explicitly throughout instruction ("Here's an example of a clarifying question you could ask a peer: 'Can someone read the question from the pink handout on your desk?'") Advocating for all of these steps during collaborative problem solving can help to ensure colleagues are providing a language-rich, appropriately supported environment. In turn, ensuring this environment, and advocating for appropriate decisions during team meetings, helps to reduce inappropriate Tier 2 and Tier 3 referrals so that students are not slated for unnecessary intervention or assessed for special education eligibility when it would be inappropriate (Ortiz et al., 2011).

Facilitating Appropriate Problem-Solving Referrals

As the educator with expertise in all of the areas described above, the ESOL teacher is in an excellent position to lead the problem-solving team in making appropriate referrals—not referring students for team consideration or special education assessment if they are simply in the process of second-language acquisition and, conversely, not ignoring genuine needs if a student presents with them. The list of reflection questions in Figure 1 can help guide teachers prior to bringing students up for team consideration or referral.

Before referring a student for team consideration or special education eligibility determination, consider whether all of the following elements of linguistically appropriate Tier 1 instruction have been provided in the general education classroom.

- Language scaffolds and supports (word banks with and without pictures, sentence stems, organizers for taking notes)
- Explicit modeling of language (e.g., how to write a lab report; how to ask questions in a discussion)
- Explicit support with language needed to access content (vocabulary, specialized phrases) in the form of explicit teaching, opportunities for practice, and written templates, models, or scaffolds (sample paragraphs, skeletal notes, organizers to fill in)
- Visuals, manipulatives, or concrete models
- Use of the home language as appropriate to provide academic support, clarify content, and encourage student speech

When observing an English learner having difficulty in the general education classroom, are the following elements present?

- Are other English learners with comparable backgrounds struggling? (If all English learners are struggling, an issue with instruction or language accessibility is more likely.)
- Are visuals and supports present in the room?
- Are structures and strategies offered to decrease the cognitive load of language processing? (For example, are vocabulary lists offered; is extended time provided; are students encouraged to use learning and metacognitive strategies as they are learning?)

Figure 1: Pre-problem-solving reflection list

Speaking to the Exclusionary Factors Rule

Finally, the ESOL teacher can play a useful role in reminding team members of the "exclusionary factors" rule (Ortiz et al, 2011) that a student's status as an EL should not be the driver of any special education determination. Teams sometimes interpret the Individuals with Disabilities Education Act of 1990 (IDEA) as limiting their ability to qualify English learners for special education under any circumstances, but this is inaccurate. Rather, students who are English learners can be qualified as having educational disabilities in certain circumstances where the team has determined their language learning needs are not the primary reason for their difficulties. The following situations are examples from our own practice that would meet this criteria:

- When a student exhibits challenges across languages
- When developmental hurdles or delays in the first languages are present
- When the student's rate of progress in learning English differs from that of ESOL peers
- When challenges exist across social and academic settings and are not attributable to cultural differences

Fundamentals of Successful Collaborative Planning

School teams are critical loci of activity for student support through which changes in policy may gain traction and show results. Implementation of evidence-based instructional practices in the classroom and staff professional development are not enough to support all learners' diverse needs. Coordination across tiers and teams to deliver supplemental instruction and interventions is critical (Fuchs & Fuchs, 2016). Most often in recent years, this coordination takes place in a response-to-intervention/multitiered systems of support-based model (Fuchs & Fuchs, 2016). In such a model, all students receive high-quality (Tier 1) general instruction. After screening is performed on all students to identify those who might be at risk, those students with instructional or behavioral needs receive targeted supports, often referred to as Tier 2 instruction or Tier 2 interventions (RTI Network, n.d.). Last, those students who have more intensive needs, or who fail to improve with Tier 2 supports, are provided more intensive, Tier 3 supports (which may or may not coincide with special education services) (Fuchs & Fuchs 2016).

The structure and collaborative nature of teaming look different from school to school, district to district, and state to state. The ESOL teacher may work in a variety of teaming situations; often, elementary teams are arranged by grade level, and secondary teams are arranged by content area. This section will focus on the collaborative structures at the school and team level that effectively meet diverse students' needs. Just as we use a developmental framework to deliver instruction and services to students, so can we apply this model to adults and teams. Teams and their members will be at different stages of understanding the populations, of building knowledge, and, in some cases, of accepting district-level changes. Identifying how to engage team members at each stage of the change process, or where they are developmentally, will help to ensure responsive practices and problem solving for all learners; well-developed processes and procedures are important for teacher growth and change (Pieters & Voogt, 2016). While backed up with current research when appropriate, I have gleaned much of what follows from my substantial experience as a district-level administrator supporting collaborative-planning structures in many diverse schools.

Team development and ESOL collaboration. Schools often rely on meetings where staff discuss students' challenges one-by-one, but a structure for systemic problem-solving or concurrent staff development is not always in place. Structured teaming, including the consistent involvement of the ESOL teacher, provides for both of these by utilizing a structured process and describing the rationale behind decisions so all team members can learn from them. Teaming, in general, requires

- Trust, equality, and respect;
- Defined roles;
- Shared purpose and commitment;
- Collective decision-making;
- Shared resources and knowledge; and
- Joint responsibility for outcomes.

Each team process differs depending upon the model of service delivery adopted by the state, district, and/or school. Under current federal education law, the Every Student Succeeds Act of 2015 (ESSA) provides guidance for school districts to implement multitiered systems of support. It does not, however, stipulate the specifics of how that should look in practice, for example, how many tiers are needed or how many students each tier of service delivery should comprise. ESSA defines a "multi-tier system of supports" as "a comprehensive continuum of evidence-based, systemic practices to support a rapid response to students' needs, with regular observation to facilitate data-based instructional decision-making" (ESSA, 2015). Similarly, federal special education law, the Individuals with Disabilities Education Act, focuses on other methods for special education identification such as the Response to Intervention Model (IDEIA, 2004). While many view RTI as synonymous with a multitiered system of support, the two differ somewhat. The latter is used to describe the model under which all academic, behavioral, and socioemotional interventions fall. RTI is viewed as the model used to help students struggling with academics. Three levels of intervention are typical, and, as students need more intensive intervention, they move through tiers of increasing intensity. The multitiered system of support in ESSA is more comprehensive and may include an RTI model; however, it moves beyond academics to cover social emotional supports.

Varied options are available for the implementation of multitiered systems of support or response to intervention, though in general two basic approaches to RTI are followed, the standard protocol model and problem-solving model (VanDerHeyden, n.d.). The main differences between the two approaches lie in how instructional decisions and placement are made and in the number of interventions used with individual students. In a problem-solving model, the team makes instructional decisions based on an individual student's performance. Struggling students are presented with a variety of interventions, based on their individual needs and performance data. In the standard protocol model, the person delivering the intervention makes instructional decisions that follow a standard protocol. Struggling students are presented with one standard, validated intervention that addresses a variety of skills. ESOL teachers bring expertise that can be used across the models, as they can guide teams to interpret student performance in light of language proficiency, consider instructional decisions in light of language skills and needs, and offer guidance about the appropriateness of interventions used in either model.

Structures for Collaborative Problem Solving: Defined Roles

Teams benefit from clearly defined roles, as this can help each team member to feel valued and support the overall goals of the team. In determining roles for team-based problem solving, team members may consider several variables: how many team members are present, how much time is allowed for discussion, how much information teachers are able to collect on their own, and what kind of support they may need from specialists or experts on the team (Friend & Cook, 2017). Table 1 suggests one potential set of roles.

Table 1 Problem-Solving Roles

Role	Function
Problem-solving coach or leader	Facilitates meeting, gathers records and data, summarizes team conclusions
Administrator	Offers guidance on building and district policies; collaboratively plans and directs instruction and intervention selections as they relate to administrator expertise
School psychologist	Can offer insight about various assessments, strategies, and behavioral interventions, particularly social skills that have been tried and were not successful
ESOL teacher	Provides expert guidance about the role of language acquisition, acculturation, and student access to curriculum and can suggest strategies for linguistically appropriate instruction and tiered interventions; provides information on how student's English language development is progressing and contextualize it in comparison to other similar EL peers

(continued on next page)

Table 1 *(continued)*

Role	Function
Special educator	Offers insight about specific learning needs, behavioral supports, and metacognitive or learning strategies for students who are at risk for having a disability; often is familiar with UDL principles and can support their implementation in the classroom
School nurse	Provides context about health and medical needs, including impact of any diagnoses (ADHD, cerebral palsy, etc.), and provides information about attendance and recent illness, if any
Grade-level teachers	Provide performance data (about academics and behavior) and context about students of concern; conduct and interpret screening and progress monitoring; identify students to discuss with team and gather premeeting data to inform discussion
Pupil personnel worker/social worker/counselor	Provides pertinent background information about family strengths and needs, student socioemotional background, and potential supports; can assist in implementing behavioral and socioemotional interventions and supports
Specialized instructional support personnel (SISP), including speech-language pathologist, occupational therapist, audiologist, physical therapist, and other professionals	Assist with interpreting specialized data and problem solving in areas of specific expertise, such as speech and language, hearing, and fine- and gross-motor skills
Other school personnel as needed (cafeteria workers, office personnel, etc.)	Offer additional information and support in implementing targeted interventions (check-in/check-out, for example) (Filter et al., 2007)
Parents	Most important members of the team; provide insight on student's home life, strengths, and goals; must give consent for formal testing
Wraparound service providers	Personnel from other agencies and community representatives who address family and student needs; provide information on available resources, treatment plan options, and progress toward desired outcomes

Norms and Process for Problem Solving

Chapter 7, on targeted support and interventions, and chapters 8 and 9, on decision-making and eligibility for English learners who may have special education needs, will address much of the substance of how to decide on the best supports for English learners. However, consistent procedures and expectations for how teams will function are helpful; while most applicable to problem solving at Tiers 1 and 2, some of the content here may also apply to decision-making and individualized education program (IEP) teams. Often, teams review prior action steps and then begin new discussions by addressing a broad initial question: "Which students are challenged in meeting behavioral or academic needs?" This question may be posed by the administration or the problem-solving coach or coordinator. Teachers who wish to raise a student for team consideration are often asked to bring supporting data (see www.tesol.org/exceptionalneeds for a sample list of recommended data) to the meeting to demonstrate a student's patterns of strengths and needs. The process for discussing individual students may vary by team or school; at some schools, all students in a particular teacher's class may be discussed first; in others, the discussion may begin with students whose needs are more intense, followed by students whose needs are less so. As students are discussed, teams should follow well-established norms for how teachers present their information or concerns, how team members offer feedback, and which person (usually the problem-solving coach or administrator) brings the discussion to closure and identifies one or more concrete action steps. Some suggestions for productive problem solving, gleaned from research and my extensive experience working with schools and individual teams around this issue, follow.

Define expectations and responsibilities clearly. It is helpful for school administration to clarify, at the outset, how teams are expected to function. This includes concrete, logistical expectations (How often do teams meet? Who should attend?) as well as expectations related to mindset and disposition (use strengths-based language; do not assume a student is unmotivated or defiant when you have not investigated underlying reasons for challenging behavior). It is also helpful to clarify responsibilities for each of the participants (see Table 1) so that staff are aware of, for example, who is expected to convene and begin the meeting; who is expected to keep time and summarize; and when team members can chime in with questions about a particular student or situation.

Set and enforce collaborative norms. Norms should govern the "how" of collaboration as well as the underlying belief systems that teachers may express during that process. The mere process of discussing a student does not, in itself, provide a collaborative framework; rather, collaboration is characterized by openness, information-sharing, and flexibility toward others' perspectives (Friend & Cook, 2017). Teams can discuss what collaboration looks like and what their norms for collaboration are. For example, should any team member jump in with suggestions or ideas when a colleague is having difficulty with a student? What parameters exist for how to critique or interrogate another colleague's instruction? What norms should govern disagreements, particularly strongly felt ones?

End meetings with summarizers and action steps. At the end of each meeting, the designated coach or administrator should identify action steps, including who is responsible and what the timeframe for completion is. Sample action steps may include: "Let's give all of the fourth-grade teachers an extra day to reteach this concept, even though the curriculum has it taking two days, and reanalyze formative assessment data after the third day," or "So Ms. Lynn will implement a graphic organizer before this lesson to preteach vocabulary and will bring back data on how the English learners in the class, as well as the class as a whole, performed after using it."

Institute accountability for implementing those action steps. If action steps are clearly formulated, with concrete deliverables, responsible parties, and deadlines, it becomes much easier to institute accountability. Indeed, in a collaborative culture, teachers may feel accountable to colleagues simply by virtue of being on the same team; accountability is a critical element of any partnership, including one aimed at helping students at risk (Friend & Cook, 2017). It is helpful to begin each meeting by reviewing the action steps from the last meeting, giving individual staff members a chance to report on progress made or new concerns that have surfaced.

Chapter 7 provides more details about particular questions and factors to consider relating to English learners with various difficulties, whether those be academic, behavioral, or both. Considering collaborative planning needs in addressing scheduling issues is also helpful. Ideally, school schedules will allow for collaborative planning time for adults and also allow for an intervention period or block for students who may need one.

Leveraging Problem Solving for Schoolwide Change

Professional development. A culture of responsive problem solving can help to build knowledge and skills through the entire school community; in fact, tiered interventions are most successful when teachers see themselves as being part of a dedicated learning community (Mundschenk & Fuchs, 2017). Formal school-based professional development is one way to build the capacity of teams and of individual teachers for supporting all learners, including those who are diverse (Hammond, 2014). The school's core leadership group can disseminate information back to grade-level or content teams, developing skills consistently within all teams by sharing the same information. Discussions at the problem-solving table, in and of themselves, can also be a rich source of professional learning. Team meetings provide excellent opportunities to develop staff knowledge and support student success. In teams, staff resistance can be addressed and belief systems can be modeled and coached. The team meeting is ideally not a place where educators recite all of the things students can't do; rather, team-based problem solving is an interactive process in which school, community, and family partners focus together on enhancing the academic achievement and functional performance of all students in educational lessons and school activities (Friend & Cook, 2017).

Dispositions and mindset. Team processes offer an excellent opportunity for all staff to develop not only student-centered, growth-focused dispositions, but also collaborative and partnership-oriented ones. Collaborative problem solving, accomplished well, requires openness and trust in one's colleagues (Friend & Cook, 2017). It also requires vulnerability; students are best served when teachers are willing to accept suggestions, try new strategies, and change their approach based on team determinations (Pieters & Voogt, 2016). Problem solving is most successful when participants enter the process with these dispositions in place; conversely, problem solving also provides a unique way to further build these dispositions. Josefina's grade-level teacher demonstrated trust in responding to suggestions from the ESOL teacher and the pupil personnel worker; she also demonstrated vulnerability in bringing her own concerns to the team for assistance. See the supplemental case study at www.tesol.org/exceptionalneeds for another example of collaborative, team-based problem solving for an English learner.

Ecological problem solving. In a strengths-based model, all stakeholders who can impact a student's well-being and success should be at the table to build a truly comprehensive picture of the student. Community partners, who often provide basic necessities and build a continuum of support outside school, are essential to this work. If schedules preclude partners being at the table, those partners can still provide written or verbal information before (or after) the meeting. In particular, collaboration with community partners outside of team meetings may be necessary to discuss children who might need more intensive services such as counseling, or whose families may need assistance with basics such housing or food. This may be particularly essential for students who are English learners, as those students may have a significant need for resources but may need specialized support to connect them to the right resources for their families' unique situations (Grant & Ray, 2013).

Summary and Conclusion

Collaborative problem solving in a team-based model is an essential element of any tiered system that provides supports to students in varying intensities. In a model truly responsive to the cultural and language needs of English learners, the ESOL teacher will be a consistent and valued member of the team, able to contribute in multiple ways that improve all team members' knowledge of linguistically accessible instruction. In fact, the ESOL teacher can be a key player in terms of focusing the team on a student's strengths and providing strategies to facilitate the use of UDL principles in the classroom. Teams rely on well-designed structures and processes, including discussion questions, observation guides, and notetaking prompts that focus on the linguistic, cultural, and developmental variables most relevant for each learner.

Questions for Team Discussion or Shared Reflection

1. Does our school have problem-solving processes in place for all learners that consider variables of language, culture, and development?

2. Does our school involve the ESOL teacher at all stages of the problem-solving process, or are there stages in which the ESOL teacher could provide more input as a member of the team?
3. Do our team discussions allow all team members to address diverse considerations, voice opinions, and thoughtfully consider data?

References

Every Student Succeeds Act of 2015. PL No. 114-95, Sec. 8002(33).

Ferlis, E., & Yaoying, X. (2016). Prereferral process with Latino English language learners with specific learning disabilities: Perceptions of English as a second language teachers. *International Journal of Multicultural Education, 18*(3), 22–39.

Filter, K. J., et al., (2007). Check in/check out: A post hoc evaluation of an efficient, secondary-level targeted intervention for reducing problem behaviors in schools. *Education and Treatment of Children, 30*(1), 69–84.

Friend, M., & Cook, L. (2017). *Interactions: Collaboration skills for school professionals.* Upper Saddle River, NJ: Pearson.

Fuchs, D., & Fuchs, L. S. (2016). Responsiveness-to-Intervention: A "systems" approach to instructional adaptation. *Theory into Practice, 55*(3), 225–233.

Grant, K., & Ray, J. (2013). *Home, school and community collaboration: Culturally responsive family engagement.* Thousand Oaks, CA: Sage.

Hammond, Z. (2014). *Culturally responsive teaching and the brain: Promoting authentic engagement and rigor among culturally and linguistically diverse students.* Thousand Oaks, CA: Corwin.

Individuals with Disabilities Education Act of 1990.

Individuals with Disabilities Education Improvement Act of 2004. 71 Fed. Reg. 46, 647.

Klingner, J., & Eppolito, A. (2014). English language learners: Differentiating between language acquisition and learning disabilities. Arlington, VA: Council for Exceptional Children. Martin-Beltran, M., & Peercy, M. M. (2014). Collaboration to teach English language learners: Opportunities for shared teacher learning. *Teachers and Teaching: Theory and Practice, 20*(6), 721–737.

Mundschenk, N. A. & Fuchs, W. W. (2016). Professional learning communities: An effective mechanism for the successful implementation and sustainability of response to intervention. SRATE Journal, 25(2), 55–63.

Ortiz, A., Robertson, P., Wilkinson, C., Liu, Y., McGhee, B., & Kushner, M. (2011). The role of bilingual education teachers in preventing inappropriate referrals of ELLs to special education: Implications for response to intervention. *Bilingual Research Journal, 34*(3), 316–333. doi:10.1080/15235882.2011.628608

Peercy, M. M., Dotter, M., & Distefano, M. (2017). "We need more consistency": Negotiating the division of labor in ESOL-mainstream teacher collaboration. *TESOL Journal, 8*(1), 215–239.

Pieters, J., & Voogt, J. (2016). Teacher learning through teacher teams: What makes learning through teacher teams successful? *Educational Research and Evaluation, 22*(3). doi/full/10.1080/13803611.2016.1247726

Ralabate, P., & Lord Nelson, L. (2017). *Culturally responsive design for English learners: The UDL approach.* Wakefield, MA: CAST Professional Publishing.

RTI Action Network. (n.d.). Developing a response to intervention plan. Retrieved from http://www.rtinetwork.org/getstarted/develop

VanDerHeyden, A. (n.d.). Approaches to RTI. Retrieved from http://www.rtinetwork.org/learn/what/approaches-to-rti

CHAPTER 6

UNIVERSAL SUPPORTS FOR ENGLISH LEARNERS AT RISK

PATRICIA RICE DORAN AND AMY K. NOGGLE

Supports for Danh—and His Family

Danh, whose family emigrated from Vietnam four years ago, is in fifth grade and has struggled recently with remaining on task and focusing during instruction. His language arts teacher first noticed this concern in October, and it soon became an issue in his other content classes as well. Danh's performance on assessments and classwork has declined, and despite being in fifth grade, he reads on an early fourth-grade level. Danh was exited from ESOL last year but continues to receive testing accommodations, and his ESOL teacher checks in periodically with his classroom teachers to see how he is doing.

At a team meeting to discuss students at risk, Danh's math teacher mentions that he is frequently drowsy during class, an observation with which his other teachers concur. After a conversation with Danh and a separate conversation with his mother, team members learn that his parents' work schedule has changed and Danh is staying up until midnight to have his mother check his math homework and his father tuck him in (both important rituals for the family).

Applying the strengths-based framework described in chapter 1, Danh's teachers confer about how best to support Danh and his parents. First, Danh has caring and involved parents who work hard to support the family, take an active interest in his schoolwork, and have the knowledge to help with homework. Second, Danh has a strong relationship with both parents and sufficient independent motivation to complete his homework alone while waiting for them to return each night. The team discusses how to support

Danh both in terms of staying awake during the day and accessing additional help with math. The guidance counselor calls Danh's parents to brainstorm other times that Danh might receive support with math. Together, they formulate a plan for Danh to check in with his math teacher during homeroom and, also, to allow him to redo homework that he completes inaccurately. This removes the stress of needing to have every assignment checked at home for accuracy. At the same time, the team recognizes that it is important for Danh to maintain a strong connection with both parents, and so they encourage him to go to bed earlier with the understanding that both his mother and father will give him a quick hug when they arrive at midnight. Last, the math teacher arranges for Danh to receive small-group support to catch up for the next four to six weeks. The team agrees to check in with both Danh and his parents in three weeks and to meet again following those check-ins so that they can fine-tune their plan as needed.

The story of Danh highlights several dilemmas common to educators working with English learners. First, just like native speakers of English, these students often have loving and involved parents who also are balancing multiple financial and logistical demands. This balancing act may create the appearance of being less than involved or less than supportive. However, taking a positive and family-centered approach requires educators to seek out additional information so that all team members have an accurate picture of a family's needs and challenges. Second, Danh's situation highlights the impact of nonacademic factors (including but not limited to sleep, living environment, and daily stressors) on school performance. A sensitive and well-informed team will problem-solve with these factors in mind, recognizing that what goes on outside school is important in determining what happens inside school. Third, problem solving, particularly for diverse learners, may involve outreach to parents and creative solutions. In previous years, brainstorming about a fifth-grader's sleeping arrangements might have been outside the intervention team's purview. However, in a student-centered, strengths-based framework that seeks to ensure every student achieves adequate growth, such problem-solving is all in a day's work. Supports for English learners may include academic, cognitive, socioemotional and behavioral, linguistic, and family interventions and resources, all implemented as part of a collaborative approach and all monitored over time to ensure they are working.

This chapter devotes particular attention to the role of Universal Design for Learning (UDL) (CAST, 2018), a framework for curriculum and instruction that integrates accessibility, support, and challenge by considering the needs of every learner. A UDL paradigm is particularly appropriate for English learners, as it allows teachers to consider their students' strengths and tailor instruction directly to those strengths (Ralabate & Nelson, 2017; Rice Doran, 2015). Furthermore, in the special education process, access to the general curriculum is an important part of the decision-making process; federal law is quite clear that students cannot be placed in special education simply by virtue of being an English learner or having a poor reading or math instructor (IDEIA, 2004). Integrating UDL into all aspects of the learning process, then, not only is a best practice but also helps teams ensure they are meeting legal requirements for current and future instruction and interventions.

Universal Supports for English Learners

No set of hard and fast guidelines exists for supporting students such as Danh. However, a few key principles are generally accepted as being important in the problem-solving and support process. These include ensuring a language-accessible curriculum; implementing UDL; and frameworks for equity and culturally sustaining pedagogy.

Language accessibility. "Language accessibility" is a general term referring to the degree to which curriculum, materials, instruction, and assessments are accessible and easily understandable. Ensuring language accessibility requires understanding of the student's individual language-related strengths and needs as well as the language demands of the curriculum. First and foremost, putting universal supports in place, as part of a multitiered system of supports (MTSS) or a response-to-intervention (RTI) process, always requires a focus on the needs and profile of the learner. For English learners, this requires us to understand the specific nature of their language-related needs as well as other factors (including those described in Table 1). These needs may include oral as well as written literacy and language skills; a clear understanding of every student's reading, writing, listening, and speaking competencies is essential. Often, perceived underachievement may arise from a set of listening demands beyond what the student is able to complete, or from writing tasks that require more English language proficiency than the student has been able to develop in their ESOL studies thus far. Teachers may find that reviewing ESOL assessment data, along with informal classroom data, is helpful; current work samples can provide a useful supplement to more formal assessment and progress monitoring data by offering a snapshot of each student's language development. (See the supplementary vignette at www.tesol.org/exceptionalneeds for an example involving a middle school student who speaks multiple languages.)

In addition to considering each student's language-related needs, educators must also consider the demands of the curriculum across subject areas—including language demands as well as academic and cognitive ones (TESOL International Association Writing Team, 2018). Teachers may wish to sit down and review textbooks, assessments and activities, and other materials, as well as being conscious of their own verbal delivery. Table 1 provides a list of common "challenge areas" for English learners, grouped by language domain (reading, writing, listening, speaking).

Table 1 Common Language-Related Challenge Areas for English Learners With and Without Disabilities

Reading:	Listening:
Decoding and phonetic similarities	Understanding native speakers' rate of speech
Grammatical structure and syntax	Auditory processing
Understanding and utilizing text features	Differentiating among homophones and homonyms
Understanding and interpreting English language conventions	Understanding idiomatic and colloquial speech
Comprehending diverse types of texts, styles, and contexts	Familiarity with register and context
Writing:	**Speaking:**
Encoding (spelling)	Word retrieval and selection
Utilizing English conventions	Speaking fluently in English as opposed to native language
Producing language with sufficient detail	Appropriate vocabulary and sentence structure
Writing fluently in English as opposed to native language	Utilizing idiomatic and colloquial speech when appropriate
Utilizing appropriate vocabulary and sentence structure	

Once teachers identify potential areas of challenge, it is recommended that ESOL and general education professionals collaborate to ensure language demands are appropriate for the student's current level of proficiency. Adapted or modified texts, along with external supports such as graphic organizers and glossaries, can help to ensure content is understandable and accessible. In addition, a language-rich environment, and opportunities for frequent oral rehearsal, can help students process others' language and refine their own language use (TESOL International Association Writing Team, 2018). Implementing steps such as these may help to provide students opportunities for success and remove barriers. Haynes and Zacarian (2010) recommend explicit vocabulary instruction and consistently engaging students with opportunities for active learning. A common practice in ESOL instruction, which has (unfortunately) not been carried over widely to general education settings, is to create language as well as content objectives (Haynes & Zacarian, 2010; Echevarria, Vogt, & Short, 2008). Language objectives specify the language-related skills students will need, and the language-related outcomes they will demonstrate, as they attain the content objective. Language objectives may focus on receptive or expressive skills and may be closely aligned to content objectives or separate from them. For instance, students will be able to use new vocabulary to describe processes for cell division, to discuss character traits using adjectives and prepositional phrases, or to write mathematical proofs that utilize mathematical terms and conventions.

Language objectives can be helpful for content and special education teachers, as well as for ESOL teachers, in that they provide a way for teachers to make explicit the language demands of a lesson. In team planning, it is often helpful for teachers to decide on common content and language objectives and then engage in backward-mapping to ensure students have the instructional support needed to meet both objectives. This is particularly important for students, including English learners, who have disabilities that may impact language skills. For example, students with autism spectrum disorders may require additional support with pragmatics and social use of language; students with learning differences may benefit from assistance with reading and writing; students with ADHD may need explicit guidance in the revision and editing process. In considering the needs mentioned in Table 1, teams will want to reflect on the possible impact of a student's disability as well as their language-learner status, including the often-complex ways in which these factors interact. For example, Mazaa, a fourth-grade student who has a traumatic brain injury and is a native speaker of Amharic, receives both special education and ESOL services. As a result of her brain injury, Mazaa demonstrates difficulty in both languages with organizing her writing, with using conventions, and with word selection, particularly involving prepositions and other function words. In addition, as a beginning English learner, Mazaa is able to make lists and short sentences in English, to follow two-step directions, and to ask and answer simple questions in English. As she continues to gain new English-language skills, team members are careful to consider her disability-related needs, offering her visual prompts for prepositional phrases and common words in English and providing her color-blocked sentence strips to help her place each word in the correct order.

If the language objective for any given lesson, or the language demands of a class in general, cannot be easily attained by the English learners in the class, that often cues teachers that additional support is needed—or that students need alternative, less linguistically demanding ways to demonstrate their learning. This concept leads us to universal design for learning as another pillar of accessible, appropriate instruction for English learners.

Universal Design for Learning. Referenced in prior chapters, UDL has roots in neuroscience and is based on the premise of equal access for all students. UDL has become not only a mainstay in the field of education but is also a mandate under some state regulatory codes. The state of Maryland, for example, has led the way in both the endorsement and incorporation of UDL principles. In May of 2010, Maryland's Governor O'Malley signed the Universal Design for Learning bill (HB 59/SB 467) into law (CAST, 2016). This bill called for the creation of a state-level UDL Task Force, whose mission was to embed UDL principles into the state's education systems. Maryland's HB 59/SB 467 marked the first state-level UDL bill in the nation; since that time, other states have followed suit with similar initiatives. In 2011, three other states had developed mission statements related to UDL, and, by 2012, all continental states and the District of Columbia referenced UDL in their curricular documents in some manner.

The Individuals with Disabilities Education Act of 1990 (IDEA) stipulates that every child with a documented disability should be educated in their "least restrictive environment," or LRE. Although the most recent version of IDEA (IDEIA, 2004) does not reference UDL specifically, it does emphasize the use of response to intervention, also conceived of more generally as a tiered-support system and sometimes linked with the multitiered system of supports framework. Under MTSS, schools implement comprehensive, tiered supports to ensure that a variety of supports (academic, behavioral, psychological, familial, and professional growth related) are available throughout the building (NASP, 2017). The Every Student Succeeds Act (ESSA, 2015) references the importance of MTSS as a part of building-level initiatives to ensure effective outcomes for all learners (NASP, 2017). The National Educational Technology Plan of 2010 was developed, in part, with UDL principles in mind and references UDL throughout, citing the numerous instances where educational technologies and UDL intersect.

Response-to-intervention and multitiered systems of support and UDL differ from one another in that RTI and MTSS are processes for designing instruction and making educational decisions, while UDL is the act of planning curriculum design with variability to maximize student success. However, RTI, MTSS, and UDL share the objective of improving educational outcomes for students with disabilities. Thus, it is logical to assume that the teacher who embraces the UDL principles will be better able to provide a least restrictive environment for their student with a disability. The UDL principles, which are described in the following section, ensure each child greater access to educational content, more variability in the way that information is presented, and response options that allows students to "show what they know" in a way that works for them.

The conceptual framework of UDL is based on three key principles: multiple means of representation, multiple means of action and expression, and multiple means of engagement (CAST, 2018). These are described here and illustrated by means of examples at www.tesol.org/exceptionalneeds.

Multiple means of representation. This is often conceptualized as the "what" of learning (CAST, 2018). How do students best acquire new information? While some may simply be able to learn through traditional methods such as listening to a teacher give oral directions for a writing activity, others may need written directions to complement the oral; some students may need even more support and may succeed when rebus pictures are paired with the written directions.

Multiple means of action and expression. This is best explained as the "how" of learning (CAST, 2018). How can students best engage with learning materials and express what they have learned? While some students may be able to recall the sequential events in a story and "report out" to their peers orally, other students may need to write these steps down on sticky notes and refer to their notes as they speak to their peers. And yet a separate group of students may succeed only when the oral demands are completely removed, thus allowing for a written response only. Flexibility in designing instruction, including classroom activities and deliverables, allows each student to show what they know in a manner that is appropriate to their strengths, growth areas, and current levels of language skill.

Multiple means of engagement. This, the "why" of learning, is the final principle of UDL (CAST, 2018). Why are some students excited about working in groups, whereas others prefer to work alone? How are students best motivated? Teachers need to consider the personalities of students (including affect, motivation, ability to sustain attention) when planning activities. Take for example the student who fidgets in his seat as he sits at group table during an hour-long science block. A teacher has designed a lesson about exploring four different types of regional soils. Instead of passing the soil containers from table to table, she asks the students to move from table to table and to make notes on clipboards about their observations at each table. Thus, the teacher is including opportunities for movement in a way that doesn't hurt any of the other students but that is certainly "good" for the student with attentional issues.

The UDL framework is particularly beneficial for English learners. Multiple guidelines and checkpoints address language support and language-related variability (CAST, 2018), particularly across the domains of representation, action, and expression. For example, UDL Checkpoint 2.1, "Clarify vocabulary and symbols," describes ways in which teachers can support vocabulary development through pre-instruction, background knowledge, and other supports. Checkpoint 2.2, "Clarify unfamiliar syntax," recommends strategies such as highlighting particularly challenging syntax structures or explicitly teaching grammatical structures such as transition words (CAST, 2018). Leveraged across content areas, the UDL guidelines and checkpoints can provide teachers a framework for incorporating increased linguistic support into instruction at all levels, whether working with beginning English learners or those at advanced proficiency (Rice Doran, 2015). In fact, UDL can complement best practices for English learners quite effectively (Ralabate & Nelson, 2017) and can support ESOL as well as content teachers in making instruction accessible across the curriculum and across the continuum of abilities, strengths, and needs (Rice Doran, 2015).

Problem solving and interventions at Tier 1 often can interface smoothly with a UDL-based approach. Incorporating multiple means of representation, action, expression, and engagement into classroom instruction is one effective way to ensure all students, especially English learners, have the opportunity to access the curriculum (Rice Doran, 2015). The challenge for classroom teachers often arises in figuring out exactly which scaffolds or forms of support are most appropriate for English learners as opposed to native speakers—and what further differentiation they might need to apply to their typical classroom routines.

As referenced earlier, the UDL guidelines are helpful for identifying ways to make the curriculum accessible to all learners. In particular, the language-based emphasis of some of the guidelines can offer specific guidance for teachers of English learners with respect to clarifying vocabulary, syntax, and information processing (CAST, 2018). In the UDL framework, the idea of offering alternatives and choices is also beneficial for English learners, as it fosters engagement and allows students to select their own preferred learning activities. Teachers can support this by teaching metacognitive skills and empowering students to recognize and select strategies that work for them. Teachers also can support students' learning by aligning instruction and interventions to language proficiency standards, such as those developed by WIDA (World-Class Instructional Design and Assessment), one of the leading English learner assessment and instructional standard-setting organizations. The WIDA Can-Do Descriptors (Board of Regents of the University of Wisconsin System, 2012a, 2012b) or other language-development standards and descriptors are a valuable resource in describing how students' language proficiency and abilities can change. The example of Samaira, found at www.tesol.org/exceptionalneeds, demonstrates how language proficiency standards and curriculum can leverage and support each other.

A final piece of the puzzle, for teachers of students such as Samaira and others, is ensuring pedagogical approaches are grounded in responsive, culturally appropriate philosophies. Culturally sustaining pedagogy is a third pillar of universal access and support for English learners, including those at risk, and is described in more detail here.

Culturally sustaining pedagogy. A third element of UDL-based practice for diverse learners involves the application of equity-based practices within the context of culturally sustaining pedagogies. In recent years, educators have given increased attention to equitable practices as a way to ensure positive outcomes for all learners, regardless of race/ethnicity, language status, gender or sexual orientation, and ability. Equity-based teaching is rooted in awareness of systemic factors, such as racial injustice and poverty, that impact students' access to education, but it also leverages proven strategies that teachers can use to level the playing field within their own classrooms (US Department of Education, 2013).

Over time, the idea of culturally sensitive, culturally responsive, and culturally competent practice has also evolved, placing new expectations on educators to not only understand students' cultures but value them and incorporate aspects of them into classroom instruction (Paris, 2012; Ladson-Billings, 2014). In recent years, new terminology has evolved emphasizing "culturally sustaining pedagogy" (Paris, 2012), an approach that further transforms cultural relevance and requires educators not only to understand and value each student's cultural difference but to maintain that difference and seek to affirm it where it may vary from traditional educational approaches. Ladson-Billings (2014) gives the example of hip-hop–based instruction as one approach that not only respects students' cultures but actively affirms ways in which those cultures might diverge from traditional academic discourse. For English learners, culturally sustaining approaches should be foundational elements in classroom practice, including implementation of UDL in a culturally affirming context (Ralabate & Nelson, 2017). Culturally sustaining approaches have added benefits for English learners with disabilities, who are already in a doubly or triply marginalized position in many classrooms and schools, and who may be further stigmatized by teachers' lack of understanding of their cultural backgrounds.

Samantha and Trey: A Teacher's Learning Curve

Consider the example of Samantha, a young, white high school language arts teacher from a middle-class background. Samantha was at first taken aback when she saw the written work that Trey, a black student from Jamaica who also has a learning difference, turned in. Trey is one of her most passionate and verbally gifted students in classroom discussions, but his written work follows none of the guidelines for essays that she had reviewed with the class just two days prior. Rather, it begins with a lengthy narrative, digresses into a personal reflection, and concludes by referencing some of his native country's beliefs and traditions. Samantha takes Trey's paper to the ESOL teacher and the special educator for feedback, assuming Trey's unusual writing structure must be the result of organizational difficulties. The ESOL teacher suggests Samantha educate herself about oral traditions and the role of storytelling and narrative in other cultures. Ready to look at Trey's paper with a changed perspective, Samantha notices, for the first time, the graceful way Trey uses metaphors throughout the paper; the skill with which he ties his closing thoughts back to his opening images; and the subtle humor in his reflection. Samantha ends up revising the assignments she gives to the class, integrating UDL by providing students options for the types of compositions they create rather than restricting them to nonfiction five-paragraph essays. She offers Trey enrichment opportunities that involve studying narratives by outstanding black and Caribbean writers, and she also gradually introduces him to essay writing to improve his range and more traditional academic skills, while encouraging him to continue developing his own voice and style through those essays. Last, wanting Trey to achieve his potential without being hindered by his learning difference, she makes sure that he has access to text-to-speech and speech-to-text software, allowing him to speak and listen (as well as to read and write), and she helps him identify revision and editing strategies that seem to work well for him.

Tier 1 Implementation: Team-Based Collaboration and General Classroom Supports

As Samantha demonstrated in being willing to reevaluate her assignments and grading criteria, effective problem solving at the Tier 1 level focused on general access requires collaboration and openness on the part of all participants. Specific elements of an effective problem-solving process, with examples where appropriate, are described here.

Setting the scene for effective problem solving. When students are not successful in the general education classroom despite careful implementation of UDL, attention to language demands and ESOL standards, and equity-based, culturally appropriate pedagogies, teams must consider steps to address further challenges. Best practices for tiered systems of intervention require teachers to carefully consider classroom data (Forman & Crystal, 2015) and require teams to consider reasons, within a holistic framework, that students may struggle. Team mindset is critical here; taking a positive, strengths-based approach, while also carefully considering data about students' needs, helps educators to identify solutions appropriate for each learner. As described in more extensive detail in chapter 2, students may experience difficulty in the general education classroom because of specific academic skills gaps, language differences, or other factors. The list in Table 2 provides a brief summary of potential barriers students may encounter.

Table 2 Potential Barriers to Student Progress: Considerations for Teams

- Food insecurity
- High mobility/frequent moving
- Family separation
- Family constellation/composition or living situation in home
- Family unemployment or lack of job security
- Sibling illness or behavioral challenges
- Health difficulties
- Lack of sleep (may be related to other home or school factors)
- Trauma
- Changes in legal or immigration status
- Limited reading fluency
- Limited English comprehension
- Inadequate exposure to subject-specific academic vocabulary
- Lack of familiarity with subject topic/context
- Acculturation issues (still in phases of adaptation to new school/culture/norms)

This list of potential considerations for teams is not exhaustive, should not be used as a checklist, and is not intended to suggest all factors listed impact all students. Rather, this is designed as a guide to support teachers in identifying and addressing potential factors impacting student performance.

Team composition and membership. Adequate discussion of these factors presenting potential challenges requires a team approach with multiple professionals at the table representing varied fields of expertise, similar to a prereferral or IEP team. Given the varied needs with which students may present, students may need support from professionals in various roles; while general and special educators are well positioned to address academic challenges, collaborative input and strategy ideas from behavioral health and family support professionals may be essential in identifying ways to support students with mental health and family needs. A list of the types of input and professionals who may be involved in determining Tier 1 supports follows (this list is not exhaustive and may vary according to each school's circumstances and each student's needs).

- Academic input (general curriculum): General educator
- Academic input (specialized strategies): Special educator
- Academic input (language based); input on culture and acculturation: ESOL teacher
- Input on skill development: Related services providers (speech, occupational therapy, physical therapy)
- Input on mental health, trauma, or (sometimes) acculturation: Behavior and mental wellness providers (counselor, social worker, school psychologist)
- Input on family communication; assistance with global challenges (across subject areas or classes): Administrator
- Health-related input: School nurse (input may not be required for every student or at every meeting)
- Family-related input: Family outreach coordinator, counselor, or pupil personnel worker

Putting Tier 1 supports into place. For students who may experience challenges related to one of these areas, problem solving and implementation of solutions at Tier 1 looks different from problem solving at Tiers 2 and 3, where more intensive supports and progress monitoring often are required. At Tier 1, educators focus on adaptations and accommodations in the general classroom rather than on formalized interventions, which are implemented later in the problem-solving process if it becomes evident that general supports are not sufficient. Fahmida's story, which follows, illustrates how Tier 1 supports and adaptations can facilitate students' success in the general education setting, as they pursue the general education curriculum without needing intensive academic supports. Note that Fahmida previously received more intensive behavioral supports; one principle of MTSS is that its structure and implementation are flexible, so that with appropriate documentation and decision-making, supports for students can be intensified or scaled back as appropriate. For Fahmida's team, her prior history means that they will begin with less intensive supports, but progress monitor carefully and proactively so that they can move quickly to more intensive interventions if needed.

Strategies for Fahmida

Fahmida is a fourth-grader whose immediate family has a history of experiencing violence; they are immigrants who entered the United States legally under an asylum claim three years ago, as a result of political and social instability in their native country. While her current living situation is safe (she lives with her aunt), Fahmida still has a history of behavioral difficulties, including impulse control, noncompletion of work, and noncompliance with adult directions, particularly during unstructured time such as recess and lunch. Last year, Fahmida had a behavior intervention plan that included de-escalation strategies and positive reinforcements. After very successful second- and third-grade years, her behavior intervention plan was discontinued, and she was successful likewise at the beginning of fourth grade. However, in recent weeks, Fahmida has failed to complete any work and has exhibited intense emotional responses, yelling and leaving her desk on three separate occasions. Fahmida saw the school counselor biweekly in second and third grade, and her teachers have shared their concerns with the counselor. While Fahmida has never been regarded as requiring special education services, her teachers are increasingly concerned not only about the impact of behaviors on her work but, more important, her emotional well-being. Her teachers meet to discuss the shift in her behavior and agree to make several changes right away. First, they refer Fahmida to the school counselor. Second, they complete an antecedent-behavior-consequence (ABC) chart to identify the antecedents or triggers for her emotional outbursts. They determine these are most likely to occur when she is settling down from lunch or outside time. They vary their schedules so that a member of the team can observe Fahmida during these times to ensure nothing is upsetting her in conversation or interactions with peers, and they also work out a way to give Fahmida a few extra minutes to calm down and transition back to schoolwork. Finally, they give Fahmida two "exit passes" per week that she can use to leave the classroom at any time and go visit the counselor. The team agrees to meet a week later to see if these supports seem to be working. If not, they agree that they will move quickly to more targeted and intensive supports.

Considering the role of culture in behavior. It is also essential for teams to be able to differentiate between behavioral challenges and behaviors that may be culturally based. Over the past few decades, extensive research has examined the way behavioral expectations are culturally situated and may be applied differently to members of different ethnic or cultural groups. Children of black/African American background, for example, are more than twice as likely to be identified as having an emotional or behavioral disorder, a phenomenon that research attributes both to implicit teacher bias and to poorly developed understanding on the part of educators of variables that may differ across cultural groups, such as eye contact, vocal volume, and physical proximity. In the same way, educators or teams may mistakenly label students as noncompliant or having challenging behavior, when the actual concern is related to inadequate understanding of directions or incomplete understanding of cultural expectations. One educator we have worked with told the story of a student, newly arrived from a refugee camp, who experienced a conflict with a classmate and brought a machete to school the next day. From the student's cultural perspective, showing one's weapon was the next logical step in a conflict, even if he did not intend to use it to harm his peer. While this action fell under the school district's policy governing dangerous weapons, it was fortunate that the school's administrators took the student's cultural background and exposure to American school norms into account when discussing appropriate consequences. On a far less drastic level, while behaviors such as inattentiveness, failure to follow directions, lack of response to teacher questions, and talking at inappropriate or unexpected times may be interpreted as noncompliant or disrespectful, they may simply be based in a student's lack of familiarity with school expectations and culture or, in fact, in teachers' implicit biases (Ford, 2016; Mazur & Rice Doran, 2010). For this reason, teams must be cognizant of all other potential explanations for students' behavior—particularly but not limited to language and cultural difference—when that behavior is unexpected or atypical. Speaking to family members, students from similar cultural backgrounds, and the student in question may help teams to gather information to determine explanations or antecedents underlying unusual or challenging behavior. This process may be as simple as a parent mentioning that a child has been going without breakfast and thereby realizing that a logical explanation exists for her first-period crankiness. It may be as complex as listening to a child describe a recent traumatic experience and realizing that her inappropriate, externalizing behaviors are the result of untreated trauma. And it may involve teachers being willing to reevaluate their own perceptions of what is "acceptable" or "unacceptable" classroom behavior. A teacher who always expects students to use quiet voices may be enforcing consistent behavioral norms, but he may also be overlooking the animated speech styles and emotion that students from some cultures bring to the learning process.

Educators can minimize the risk of such misunderstandings by working with all students, particularly those who are English learners, to explicitly teach, model, and reinforce any behavioral expectation, throughout all grade levels, even before students evidence any difficulties. Such instruction should be provided in a manner accessible to all language learners, by modeling extensively, instructing explicitly and directly, and checking for understanding prior to enforcing behavioral norms.

Summary and Conclusion

The fundamental characteristic of effective Tier 1 instruction is a willingness, on the part of all personnel, to assume responsibility for each learner's progress. When a student encounters difficulty, whether he or she is an English learner or not, school personnel must first look at their curriculum and manner of instruction to ensure it is accessible, relevant, and appropriate. They should then consider individual student factors that may be impacting the student's progress. Some of these factors may be external, such as family pressures; some may be internal, such as a student's undiagnosed disability. Before implementing structured, targeted interventions or assessing for disabilities, teams should consider informal supports for the student as well as reevaluate the quality of content and ESOL instruction to ensure both are truly meeting the student's needs. A well-structured problem-solving process, including the presence of all appropriate personnel and consideration of appropriate data points, will help educators to identify the right supports and put them into place efficiently.

Questions for Team Discussion or Shared Reflection

1. Does our team (or our school) effectively implement UDL-based practice, culturally sustaining pedagogy, and language-accessible instruction? Do we have, or do we need, adequate professional development in each of these areas?
2. Does our team (or our school) consider all aspects of a student's life and background in identifying potential areas for supports? If not, are there aspects that we consistently seem to overlook?
3. When a student is struggling, do we have processes in place to decide who should be part of the problem-solving discussion, to guide the discussion, and to help determine what data are most relevant?
4. When a student is struggling, how do we determine what supports might best fit their linguistic and cultural background? Do we implement the same supports for all students, or do we differentiate according to language accessibility and other factors?

References

Board of Regents of the University of Wisconsin System (2012a). *WIDA English learner can-do booklet, grades 3–5*. Madison, WI: Author.

Board of Regents of the University of Wisconsin System (2012b). *WIDA English learner can-do booklet, grades 6–8*. Madison, WI: Author.

Center for Applied Special Technology (CAST). (2016). *References to UDL in public policy*. (Policy brief). Retrieved from http://www.cast.org/work-with-us/udl-public-policy.html#.W74DoHtKhhE

Center for Applied Special Technology (CAST). (2018). Universal Design for Learning guidelines version 2.2. Retrieved from http://udlguidelines.cast.org

Echevarria, J., Vogt, M., & Short, D. (2008). *Making content comprehensible for English learners: The SIOP Model*. Boston: Pearson/Allyn & Bacon.

Every Student Succeeds Act (ESSA) of 2015 (2015). Pub. No. 114-95 114 Stat. 1177 §§ 1002–9013 (2015–2016).

Ford, J. E. (2016). The root of discipline disparities. *Educational Leadership, 74*(3), 42ff.

Forman, S. G., & Crystal, C. D. (2015). Systems consultation for multitiered systems of supports (MTSS): Implementation issues. *Journal of Educational & Psychological Consultation, 25*(2–3), 276–285.

Ladson-Billings, G. (2014). Culturally relevant pedagogy 2.0: a.k.a. the remix. *Harvard Educational Review, 84*(1), 74–84.

Haynes, J., & Zacarian, D. (2010). *Teaching English language learners across the content areas*. Alexandria, VA: ASCD.

Individuals with Disabilities Education Improvement Act. (IDEIA, 2004). Bethesda, MD: ProQuest.

Individuals with Disabilities Education Act. (IDEA, 1990).

Mazur, A., & Rice Doran, P. (2010). *Teaching diverse learners: Principles for best practice*. Thousand Oaks, CA: Corwin.

National Association of School Psychologists (NASP). (2017). *Leveraging essential school practices, ESSA, MTSS, and the NASP practice model: A crosswalk to help every school and student succeed*. (Policy brief). Bethesda, MD: Author.

National Center on Universal Design for Learning (2011).

Paris, D. (2012). Culturally sustaining pedagogy: A needed change in stance, terminology, and practice. *Educational Researcher, 41*(3), 93–97. doi: http://dx.doi.org/10.3102/0013189X12441244

Ralabate, P. K., & Nelson, L. L. (2017). *Culturally responsive design for English learners: The UDL approach*. Wakefield, MA: CAST Professional Publishing.

Rice Doran, P. (2015) Language accessibility in the classroom: How UDL can promote success for linguistically diverse learners. *Exceptionality Education International, 25*(3), 1–12. Retrieved from http://ir.lib.uwo.ca/eei/vol25/iss3/1

TESOL International Association Writing Team. (2018). *The six principles for exemplary teaching of English learners*. Annapolis Junction, MD: TESOL Press.

US Department of Education. (2013). *For each and every child—A strategy for education equity and excellence*. Washington, DC: Author.

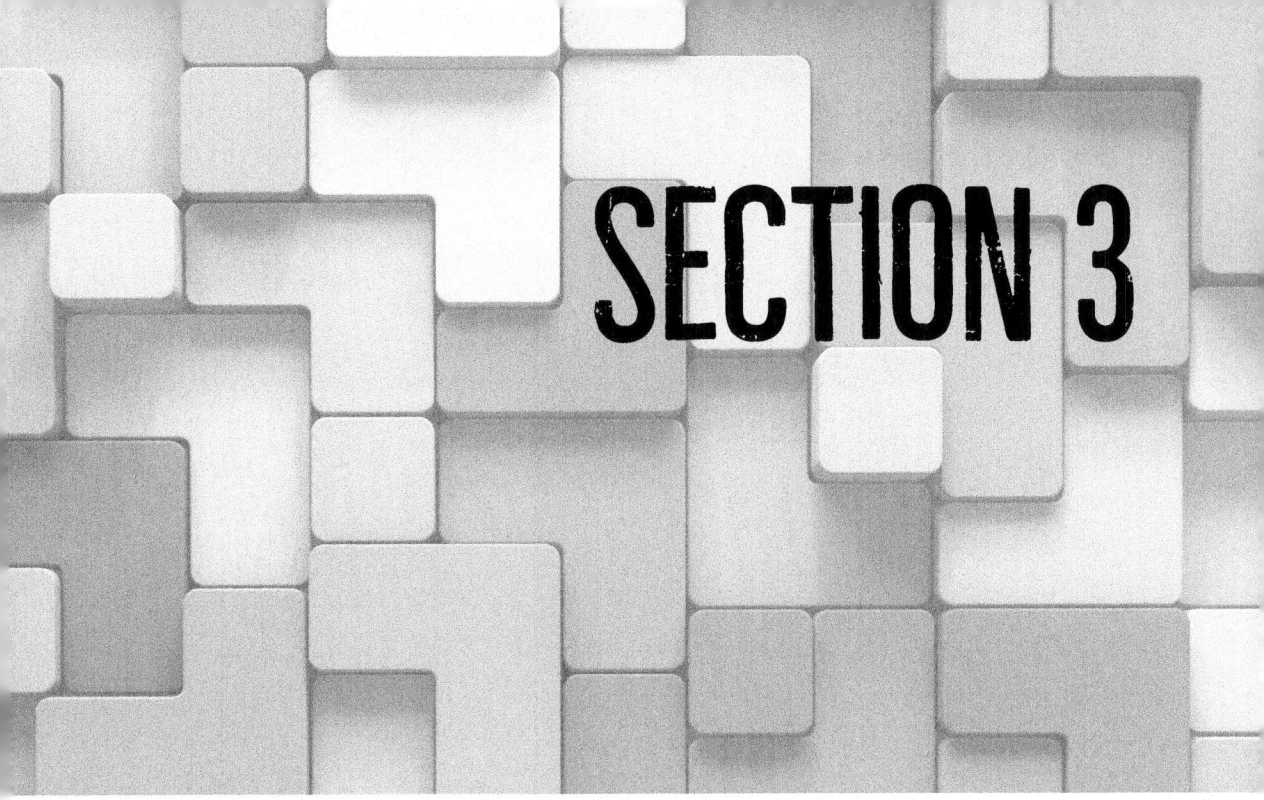

SECTION 3

SUPPORTS FOR ENGLISH LEARNERS WITH DISABILITIES

CHAPTER 7

TARGETED SUPPORTS FOR ENGLISH LEARNERS

PATRICIA RICE DORAN AND DANIELLE TURNER

What a Difference a Team Makes

Let's trace the trajectory of Lara, an English learner in fourth grade, through two hypothetical teams and schools that take two very different approaches to problem solving and targeted supports.

Team 1: Lara is an English learner at intermediate proficiency. She is in the fourth grade and reads on a second-grade level. In particular, assessment data indicate she has challenges in multiple domains of reading, including phonological awareness, fluency, and comprehension. The problem-solving team at Lara's school decided to defer reading intervention during her second- and third-grade years to give her time to "catch up" in English, although she read slightly below grade level in her native language as well. Lara has not made progress in either native language or English commensurate with expectations for her grade level and age. In fourth grade, the team initiates an English-language intervention, not normed on English learners, that focuses on phonics and fluency. They progress monitor in English every four weeks without corresponding analysis of her native language or her comprehension. Lara continues to struggle and eventually is retained in fourth grade due to lack of progress in reading.

Team 2: Lara is an English learner at intermediate proficiency in fourth grade. She was first identified with reading challenges in second grade, when curriculum-based measurements flagged her as having needs in phonological awareness, fluency, and comprehension in both languages. The second-grade team first met with Lara's parents to gain more background knowledge about her family situation, her prior educational history, and her parents' goals for their daughter. Following this meeting, they provided Lara intensive intervention in both English and her native language. The English intervention, normed on a population that included English learners, focused on fluency and phonological awareness to ensure her familiarity with the English sound system, and she received corresponding interventions in comprehension in her native language, so that she could engage in more complex cognitive tasks in her more advanced language. Teachers interpreted the English progress monitoring data with care, recognizing that Lara's performance as an English learner might differ from the benchmarks created with native English speakers in mind. Two years later, as a fourth-grade English learner, Lara is at grade level in her native language and about three months below grade level in English.

As Lara's case indicates, finding appropriate interventions for English learners at risk for having disabilities is more involved than simply opening a guide to instructional programs and picking one that seems like a good fit. Lara's team, in the second scenario, paid attention to her personal and linguistic background, her language and literacy needs, and her academic achievement as measured by reliable, linguistically valid progress monitoring. This approach allowed team members to accurately identify not only when Lara needed support, but how best to provide it and how to make sure it was effective.

In this chapter, we will review parameters for providing targeted supports and interventions to English learners (often referred to as Tier 2 Intervention in a response-to-intervention [RTI] or multitiered system of supports [MTSS] paradigm). As a reminder, Tier 2 interventions and supports are typically provided to students at risk who demonstrate academic or behavioral needs but who have not yet qualified for special education services. As intervention programs can vary widely based on district resources, student needs, and language considerations, we will not present a discrete list of recommended interventions; rather, we will review considerations for selecting, implementing, and monitoring interventions so that personnel can appropriately select from among whatever options are available in their district. As we will discuss, the ESOL teacher plays—or should play—a critical role in this process.

Identifying Students in Need of Targeted Support

Chapter 5 presented an overview of the collaborative problem-solving process for English learners. One outcome (though not the only one) of that process is the ability to identify, with reliability and cultural appropriateness, students who may need targeted support. A collaborative problem-solving process is typically the preferred way to identify those students who may need tiered intervention. It is based on authentic data rather than on formal assessments alone; it allows for input from multiple personnel; and it allows teams to meet, consider data, and adjust decisions over time. Strong Tier 2 processes, in fact, are critical for making appropriate special education decisions, as they generate robust and reliable data that reflect actual classroom performance that teams can use to qualify students for special education services if needed. Tier 2 processes also allow students to receive assistance sooner than they otherwise might and teams to evaluate whether and how specific interventions affect a student's general functioning. See www.tesol.org/exceptionalneeds for a brief review of elements involved in the collaborative problem-solving process.

Decisions About Targeted Supports

Decisions about targeted supports for English learners should be particularly nuanced with respect to language, culture, prior schooling, and literacy, as disproportionate referral to intervention is possible when decisions are not culturally and linguistically sound (Cramer, 2015). Prior experience, particularly trauma, may also be a factor. In one study, members of collaborative problem-solving teams indicated that while they often considered English proficiency, they rarely considered native-language literacy or proficiency and socioemotional variables when making decisions about interventions (Rice Doran, 2016). This approach can lead to delayed identification, inappropriate placement or services, and inefficient instruction. For this reason, appropriate intervention must start with awareness of students' needs, strengths, and unique profiles. For example, a team might build an intervention around a student's diagnosed phonics needs but also integrate her interest in roller skating by giving her passages to read related to skating or providing skating-themed stickers as incentives. In a more complex situation, a team might consider phonics intervention for a struggling reader but decide, after considering the very different sound system of the student's native language, that Tier 2 intervention would be counterproductive at that point, and more time, combined with careful progress monitoring, would be a linguistically appropriate way to meet the student's needs.

Please refer to www.tesol.org/exceptionalneeds for a list of some common variables that may impact performance for English learners. Teams should consider all of these when analyzing data and identifying potential interventions. See www.tesol.org/exceptionalneeds for a discussion of how an accurate understanding of the reasons underlying behavior made a crucial difference for one student, Akemi.

It is critically important to know a student's full history and select interventions carefully, particularly for students from diverse backgrounds (Rice Doran, Mazur, & Llagas, 2012). Regardless of evidence base or cultural appropriateness, no behavioral intervention would have worked for Akemi because her problem was medical, not behavioral. Having a collaborative, multidisciplinary problem-solving process, as discussed in chapter 5, can help to avoid such instances of mismatched interventions. School psychologists, counselors, general and special educators, ESOL personnel, social workers or pupil personnel workers, and school nurses all have important questions to ask and perspectives to contribute—and all can suggest interventions or supports from different vantage points.

The questions listed in the strengths and needs guide found at www.tesol.org/exceptionalneeds may help teams distinguish among potential causes of student difficulty and suggest appropriate interventions. Interventions for English learners should address language, social, cultural, and cognitive considerations. In particular, language difference may impact screening or progress monitoring results with respect to reading, writing, math, and even behavior. Some common areas of impact are described here.

Reading. Several excellent recent books, including Hoover, Baca, and Klingner's *Why do English learners struggle with reading?* (2016) and Pandey's *Language building blocks: Essential linguistics for early childhood educators* (2012), address specific elements of reading and literacy instruction and intervention for English learners. As a rule, teams should consider how the process of language acquisition may impact literacy development or a student's ability to demonstrate specific skills. A brief discussion of the elements of literacy, and how they relate to English learners' development, follows.

Phonological awareness and phonics. Interventions for English learners may address both native-language and English sound systems and sound-symbol correspondence. Ideally, personnel providing interventions will be familiar with the native-language sound system. When screening English learners for phonological or phonemic issues, personnel should refer to the sound and symbolic system of the first language (L1) and should cross-check any errors made on the screening assessment to be sure that they do not stem simply from familiarity with the native language. In addition, interventions targeting phonological awareness or decoding should, to the extent possible, make use of the student's existing native-language skills, as language and literacy knowledge transfers from the native language to others (Cummins, 2007). Recent research demonstrates correlations between native-language phonemic awareness and vocabulary and acquisition of English reading skills (Kelley, Roe, Blanchard, & Atwill, 2015).

Fluency. Some educators may use fluency as a proxy for comprehension, as strong fluency is often a necessary component of strong overall reading skills, and it increases the amount of text a student can successfully comprehend. This assumption, however, is especially problematic for English learners, who may have well-developed fluency in L1 and may be able to transfer that fairly easily to English if the sound-symbol systems are similar. Teachers should use caution in making instructional decisions based solely on fluency for English learners (Vanderwood, Tung, & Checca, 2014). Fluency progress monitoring instruments, in particular, should be normed on English learners and constructed in a way that ensures culturally appropriate content. Fluency scores should not be considered a proxy for comprehension in English learners unless extensive previous data gathered from the student indicates an association between the two.

Rocco's Reading Fluency

Rocco is a third-grader who is a recent emigrant from Italy. As his father is a native Spanish speaker, Rocco is fluent in Spanish as well as English, and he code-switches between the two languages with skill. Rocco is a beginning-level English learner according to his county's ESOL intake assessment. However, his reading teacher consistently reports that his reading fluency is outstanding. In fact, she had placed Rocco in the most advanced reading group based solely on an oral running record. She found, however, that Rocco's performance level changed significantly when she integrated some comprehension questions after the oral reading portion. As it turned out, Rocco's oral reading skills are excellent because of his strong language background and his well-developed native-language literacy. However, his English-language background is not sufficient to support his placement in the highest reading group, and his teacher changes his placement so that he can focus on attaining comprehension skills commensurate with his reading fluency. By fifth grade, Rocco's comprehension in English will improve significantly, and he will once again be placed in the most advanced reading group in the grade.

Vocabulary. For English learners, vocabulary incorporates both everyday words from the everyday lexicon (basic interpersonal communicative skills, or BICS) and also complex and academic language (cognitive academic language proficiency, or CALP) (Cummins, 2007; Cummins, 2008). Everyday BICS-style vocabulary (Cummins, 2008) is acquired through the normal course of daily activities and, unless a student has receptive or expressive language challenges, is often picked up relatively quickly (Cummins, 2008). Academic language, on the other hand, constitutes an area of ongoing need for many English learners (Short & Echevarria, 2016), and it may be especially productive to provide interventions focusing on subject-specific vocabulary and specific features of school-based language. These may also include sentence starters or question stems, such as those taught within the Accountable Talk paradigm (Fisher, Rothenberg, & Frey, 2008). Prior educational experience can influence whether a student brings existing academic language and vocabulary, in either language, to the classroom. To maximize vocabulary learning, content-area teachers are encouraged to collaborate with ESOL teachers and to utilize some of the instructional methodologies used in ESOL. For example, building on kinesthetic learning strategies and having students engage in whole-body response inspired by using the total physical response (Asher, 2003) approach can be both engaging and helpful to English language learning. Pointing out, and purposefully using, cognates from the native language may be useful also (August, Carlo, Dressler, & Snow, 2005). Finally, strategies that leverage conceptual elements of vocabulary, such as semantic maps and semantic feature analysis, can be used as informal interventions with English learners (see www.tesol.org/exceptionalneeds for an example illustrating the use of semantic feature analysis as a vocabulary intervention).

Comprehension. Comprehension is frequently an area of challenge for English learners (Hoover, Baca, & Klingner, 2016). Comprehension relies on strong decoding, fluency, and vocabulary skills and also requires students to be aware of the cultural and social context of what they are reading. Interventions focused on comprehension should allow students to make use of native or additional languages to support language processing, recall, inferential reasoning, and elaboration. Collaborative strategic reading (CSR), reciprocal teaching, and peer-assisted learning strategies (PALS) are particular evidence-based approaches that incorporate oral language and peer interaction (O'Connor & Vadasy, 2011). These can be implemented on a daily or weekly basis as part of general whole-class instruction, or they can be implemented with small groups for more targeted intervention. Pragmatic and social context may also play a role in students' comprehension of text; reviewing instructional and assessment texts for cultural match should be one of the first steps in lesson planning. Visit www.tesol.org/exceptionalneeds, for further examples and suggestions for determining whether a given text is culturally appropriate.

Writing.

Written expression. In supporting English learners with writing fluency and expression challenges, teams should first pay attention to native-language fluency as well as developing English proficiency. Like other language skills, writing fluency often transfers from the native language. Students scoring below expectations on measures of writing fluency may be in early stages of language acquisition and may benefit from more time or opportunities for oral practice and fewer mechanical corrections until greater language proficiency is attained. English learners may bring strong writing abilities in their first language or languages. In addition, they may bring meaningful experiences that they are eager to share (and that may enrich the classroom and school!). Like other aspects of literacy, written expression can transfer from one language to another, so teachers can leverage native-language skills in teaching English writing: "We are going to write a topic sentence with three supporting details. Let's do our prewriting in a language that you choose, then draw a picture. Then, you can talk your classmate through your picture and, when you are ready, you can write your paragraph." To assess fluency and expression in both languages, teachers might also consider allowing students to write in both the native language and English.

Mechanics. English learners in early stages of language acquisition are unlikely to have strong command of grammatical rules, including syntax, punctuation, and spelling. Waiting for these students to develop language proficiency, while providing meaningful opportunities for practice and oral language use, is likely to be more productive than intensive early intervention in mechanics. Teachers may appropriately select a few conventions essential for meaning (initial-letter capitalization, end-of-sentence punctuation) and teach these along with foundational writing skills that students are mastering. However, full-scale intervention in mechanics is likely inappropriate for beginning English learners. Looking into student's backgrounds and language experiences before selecting or designing a writing intervention can be of great value.

Native-Language Literacy for Omer

Omer is a quiet and artistic third-grade student who immigrated to the United States from Turkey with his parents soon after his birth. His parents are literate in Turkish, Kurmanji (northern Kurdish dialect), and English. During an interest inventory, he told his teacher, Ms. Evans, that he learned to read from his mother, who has always read stories aloud to him before bed. Omer is able to read aloud at an accelerated rate similar to that of a middle-school student. However, his teacher is concerned that he reads through punctuation, and although he understands implicit elements of the text, often cannot recall explicitly stated information from what he's read. Omer's tendency to omit punctuation while reading aloud is mirrored in his writing, in which capitalization and punctuation are regularly not present. When Omer is given the choice to write in his native language or English, he chooses to write in English, and eventually Ms. Evans learned that Omer was never formally taught to write or read in Turkish or in Kurdish dialect. His parents' emphasis on reading in English and his natural abilities are likely the reasons for his advanced reading rate and implicit understanding of the text's meaning. Still, his lack of practice with writing in his native language has caused gaps in his development as a writer.

His teacher develops a plan to help Omer gain experience reading and writing in Turkish. After a little searching online, Ms. Evans finds some developmentally appropriate books in Turkish as well as English and works with the ESOL teacher to purchase a selection for the school's library. Ms. Evans shares a variety of wordless picture books with Omer as well. After he reads these books at home and at school, she instructs him to write about the story he read or create a story of his own from the pictures in the wordless picture books, using either language. After sharing his writing with his parents, who are able to discuss it with him in multiple languages, he produces a final expanded and edited version in English. This adapted writing process helps Omer produce a bilingual Writing Workshop journal where he gains practice developing his ideas first in his native oral language and then translating them to English. In addition, by consistently using punctuation in the revision and editing process, Omer becomes more aware of punctuation when he reads aloud in English. His reading rate slows slightly to allow for the natural pausing that punctuation requires, and his ability to recall explicit details from the text improves as well.

Perhaps with less follow-up on Ms. Evans' behalf, she might have assumed that Omer had a great deal of experience reading and writing in Turkish, his first language. Yet assumptions about bilingual students' literacy experiences in their native language can limit teachers' instructional decision-making. Privileging students' actual experiences, those expressed by the students' and shared by their families, prevents such assumptions from influencing instruction. Surveying students and their families are a vital way for teachers to gain information about the individual strengths and needs of each student.

Mathematics.

Literacy and language demands. Often described as the "universal language," math is often anything but universal. In identifying potential interventions to support math skills, teams need to be mindful of the language demands of those interventions. For example, is the vocabulary accessible to an English learner at various levels? Are new terms explained clearly, with multisensory and graphic support as needed? What is the length and syntactic complexity of word problems and explanations? Are students offered enough context to grasp the pragmatic dimensions of problems? Any attempt to provide math intervention to English learners must be based on appropriate assessment data demonstrating gaps in mathematical knowledge rather than on differences in language processing, vocabulary, or academic language, which are particularly challenging for English learners (National Academies of Sciences, Engineering, and Medicine, 2017). Additionally, language processing often takes extra time and cognitive resources; intervention programs in math, particularly those that are computerized and utilize timed problem solving, should take this processing difference into account. In fact, well-developed computerized mathematics interventions should be able to incorporate many of a student's recommended or required language-learning accommodations, including extra time, vocabulary support, or use of a bilingual dictionary. Providing a mathematics intervention that lacks language accessibility is counterproductive and will lead to invalid progress monitoring data and, therefore, inappropriate decision-making. As in other areas, ESOL teachers are particularly well positioned to advocate for appropriate mathematics interventions and to educate team members about how to make decisions if appropriate interventions have not been provided.

Cultural context. As with other interventions, programs and materials in mathematics must take students' cultural backgrounds into account (Klingner & Edwards, 2006). Cultural mismatch or bias in materials can lead to students having difficulty accessing the content; in addition, cultural mismatch in delivery or learning modality (excessive reliance on individual work for students from group-oriented cultures, for example) can lead to students having difficulty learning or demonstrating what they know.

Behavior. In the past, more resources addressing literacy and language needs for English learners than those addressing behavior have been available to teachers. With recent research on the role of trauma in learning, some researchers are paying new attention to English learners' behavioral needs (Haynes & Zacarian, 2015). Increasing numbers of students arrive in schools as refugees from war zones or violent areas, and some students experience chronic stress during the transition to the US school system or while helping their families navigate daily life (Haynes & Zacarian 2015). Such experiences can impact student behavior. Haynes & Zacarian recommend using structured routines in the classroom, ready access to services, and collaboration between providers (such as the ESOL teacher and the social worker or pupil personnel worker). Understanding students' backgrounds and working collaboratively to match families as well as students with appropriate services is extremely important.

Bassam's Transition to School

Bassam, along with his family, was a recent immigrant having his first experience in a traditional school. His family, who had originally been farmers in Syria, was displaced by civil war and spent two years in refugee camps before being resettled in the United States. In the second week of school, Bassam becomes involved in a heated argument with another student, who made fun of his performance in four-square and insulted his family. The next day, Bassam brings a machete to school in his backpack and shows it to a friend, confiding that he is prepared to defend himself and his family's honor. The friend informs a teacher, who alerts school administration. When questioned, Bassam readily shows the principal his machete and indicates he did not realize he was not allowed to carry it with him. In accordance with protocol, school administration calls law enforcement as well as Bassam's family, and the principal has a lengthy discussion with the police officers who respond, explaining Bassam's background and home culture. Bassam's school district had recently moved away from zero-tolerance policies, and school and district administrators work carefully with Bassam and his family to ensure that he understands the nature of US schools and the importance of school safety, including bans on weapons. School administrators also work to provide Bassam with in-school counseling and to connect his family with resources that might help them address stress, trauma, and acculturation as they settle into their new community. (See www.tesol.org/exceptionalneeds for further recommendations for engaging families in intervention planning.)

A recent study (Ash, Rice, & Redmond, 2014) indicates English learners typically perform lower on measures of sociability and shyness when assessed solely in English. Students' sociability and peer relationships improved when measured in native languages as well as English. While such a finding may not surprise ESOL teachers, it is a useful reminder that English learners' language processing, both receptive and expressive, and acculturation processes may significantly impact how teachers perceive their behavior. As described in chapters 2 and 4, a school's cultural and ecological context may have a great deal to do with students' comfort levels and social behaviors. Therefore, particularly for English learners, teams must consider each student's social and cultural background, current emotional needs, and language proficiency—both receptive and expressive—in deciding whether behavioral interventions are appropriate and determining what those might be. In selecting any behavioral or social intervention, including social-skills training, the team should work with the ESOL teacher to ensure that students have the expressive and receptive language and the socioemotional availability to participate. Students who lack the language skills to access a behavioral intervention need a different intervention.

Implementing Appropriate Interventions

As discussed earlier, teams should work collaboratively to ensure that intervention decisions are culturally and linguistically appropriate. Interventions must be normed on English learners, designed for English learners, or designed to be accessible to English learners. To ensure fidelity of implementation, interventions must be delivered as designed; if customization is necessary (increasing wait time, changing the language in which the intervention is delivered, etc.), results should be interpreted accordingly. When interventions or progress monitoring tools are modified to improve linguistic accessibility for English learners, teams cannot use the original scoring norms to determine progress as those norms do not apply to modified instruments.

Collaborating between ESOL teachers and other staff. ESOL teachers, traditionally, have not been involved in selecting reading interventions or determining special education services for students. However, for students receiving Tier 2 interventions, the involvement of the ESOL teacher is critical. Teams should ensure that the ESOL teacher is present at any meeting where intervention decisions are to be made. Teams should also ensure that, at a minimum, the ESOL teacher provides input on intervention materials, progress monitoring instruments, and the methods used to analyze progress monitoring data and make decisions. Such collaboration may be challenging in schools where the ESOL teacher is itinerant or has a high workload. See www.tesol.org/exceptionalneeds for some practical workarounds to logistical and time issues that may pose a challenge to the ESOL teacher's involvement.

Progress monitoring/evaluating effectiveness. Effectiveness of a targeted intervention may be determined by a change in the student's rate of growth, attainment of a specific benchmark, or both, allowing educators to select the most appropriate means of determining progress for a given population (Fuchs & Fuchs, 2006). For English learners, criteria for expected progress should be carefully considered in light of language, culture, and expected rate of progress for an English learner peer group. Here are some questions for teams to consider in monitoring progress:

- Is the same measure or assessment used to monitor progress for English learners and non-English learners? If not (for example, if a native-language reading prompt is used to monitor comprehension skills), is the team looking carefully at student data to ensure both instruments are valid?
- Is "progress" defined as attainment of a benchmark, change in the rate of growth, or both?
- Is it anticipated that language-learning processes, or cultural differences, might change a student's rate of progress or growth on this measure? If so, has the ESOL teacher provided information to the team on specific differences for English learners?
- Does "acceptable progress" on this measure look different for an English learner as opposed to a native speaker of English? If not, is the language-learning process addressed anywhere in the intervention, or are accommodations provided? If the team decides "acceptable progress" should be measured differently for English learners, is the team taking steps to ensure equity and maintain high expectations for English learners?
- Are parents being informed about the intervention, any changes in student learning or growth, and follow-up team conversations about this student?

Summary and Conclusion

Selecting, implementing, and monitoring interventions for English learners require thoughtful consideration as well as collaboration. While a plethora of research-based interventions may exist in the marketplace, many of these may be inappropriate for English learners. Those that are culturally and linguistically sensitive may yet have been normed on native speakers, making it challenging to monitor progress. Regardless of the area selected for intervention, teams need to identify appropriate ways to interpret data and use it for decision-making. Throughout the intervention process, as with all educational activities, parents and family members should not only be at the table but also be invited to speak with authority about their student.

Questions for Team Discussion or Shared Reflection

1. Does our problem-solving process take into account students' native language and literacy, socioemotional background, and other factors that may influence performance?
2. Do we have reading, writing, math, and behavior interventions that are appropriate for English learners?
3. How do we follow up in monitoring progress after a student begins receiving an intervention?
4. If a student is not making progress, do we have culturally and linguistically appropriate processes for determining what steps might be appropriate as follow-up?

References

Ash, A. C., Rice, M. L., & Redmond, S. M. (2014). Effects of language context on ratings of shy and unsociable behaviors in English language learning children. *Language, Speech, and Hearing Services in Schools, 45*(1), 52–66.

Asher, J. (2003). *Learning another language through actions* (6th ed.). Los Gatos, CA: Sky Oaks Productions, Inc.

August, S., Carlo, M., Dressler, C., & Snow, C. (2005). The critical role of vocabulary development for English language learners. *Learning Disabilities Research and Practice, 20*(1), 50–57.

Cramer, L. (2015). Inequities of intervention among culturally and linguistically diverse students. *Penn GSE Perspectives on Urban Education, 12*(1).

Cummins, J. (2007). Rethinking monolingual instructional strategies in multilingual classrooms. *Canadian Journal of Applied Linguistics (CJAL)/Revue Canadienne de Linguistique Appliquée (RCLA), 10*(2), 221–240.

Cummins, J. (2008). BICS and CALP: Empirical and theoretical status of the distinction. In B. Street & N. H. Hornberger (Eds.), *Encyclopedia of Language and Education, Volume 2: Literacy* (2nd ed., pp. 71–83). New York: Springer Science + Business Media LLC.

Fisher, D., Rothenberg, C., & Frey, N. (2008). *Content-area conversations: How to plan discussion-based lessons for diverse language learners*. Alexandria, VA: ASCD.

Fuchs, D., & Fuchs, L. S. 2006. Introduction to responsiveness-to-intervention: What, why, and how valid is it?. *Reading Research Quarterly, 41*(1), 93–99, https://www.uv.uio.no/forskning/om/helga-eng-forelesning/introduction-to-responsivenes-to-intervention.pdf

Haynes, J., & Zacarian, D. (2015). English learners living with trauma, violence and chronic stress. [Blog post]. Retrieved from http://blog.tesol.org/els-living-with-trauma-violence-and-chronic-stress/#more-5250

Hoover, J., Baca, L., & Klingner, J. (2016). *Why do English learners struggle with reading?* Thousand Oaks, CA: Corwin.

Kelley, M., Roe, M., Blanchard, J., & Atwill, K. (2015). The influence of Spanish vocabulary and phonemic awareness on beginning English reading development: A three-year (K–2nd) longitudinal study. *Journal of Research in Childhood Education, 29*(1), 42–59.

Klingner, J., & Edwards, P. (2006). Cultural considerations with response to intervention models. *Reading Research Quarterly, 41*(1), 108–117.

National Academies of Sciences, Engineering, and Medicine (2017). *Promoting the educational success of children and youth learning English: Promising futures.* doi.org/10.17226/24677

O'Connor, R., & Vadasy, P. (2011). *Handbook of reading interventions.* New York, NY: Guilford Press.

Pandey, A. (2012). *Language building blocks: Essential linguistics for early childhood educators.* New York, NY: Teachers' College Press.

Rice Doran, P. (2016). Teachers' self-reported knowledge regarding English learners: Perspectives on culturally and linguistically inclusive instruction and intervention. *International Journal of Inclusive Education, 21*(5), 557–572.

Rice Doran, P., Mazur, A., & Llagas, C. (2012). Factors influencing needs of young dual-language learners and their families. *Young Exceptional Children Monograph Series 14: Supporting young children who are dual language learners with or at risk for disabilities.* Arlington, VA: Council for Exceptional Children.

Short, D., & Echevarria, J. (2016). *Developing academic language with the SIOP model.* Upper Saddle River, NJ: Pearson.

Vanderwood, M. L., Tung, C., & Checca, C. (2014). Application of a multitiered system of support with English language learners. *International Journal of School & Educational Psychology, 2*(1), 45–53.

CHAPTER 8

ASSESSMENT AND IDENTIFICATION FOR ENGLISH/ CULTURALLY AND LINGUISTICALLY DIVERSE LEARNERS: HIGH-INCIDENCE DISABILITIES

PATRICIA RICE DORAN AND AMY K. NOGGLE

Tomiwa's Transition

Tomiwa (Tomi for short) is a 7-year-old boy in Ms. Veretta's first-grade class. Tomi was born with Down syndrome in his home country of Benin. He moved to the United States with his parents when he was 4 years old. At that time, he was referred to Child Find by the family's new pediatrician. Tomi's family speaks Yoruba, which is certainly not as common as other foreign languages spoken in the United States; thus, finding adequate testing instruments, along with interpreters, is a notable challenge. The school team tries to find a Yoruban interpreter within the timeframe mandated by the Individuals with Disabilities Education Act of 2004 with no luck. With some hesitation, they ask Tomi's aunt, who is also a social worker and was recommended by several people in the community, to interpret during the series of testing sessions. After compiling the most accurate information possible, the school team determines that Tomi has an intellectual disability (ID). His score on the Woodcock Johnson (WJ-IV) Test of Cognitive Abilities indicates that his composite IQ score is a 68. A popular test of receptive language, the Peabody Picture Vocabulary Test (PPVT-4) indicates that his score is in the mid-70s. Adaptive scores on the Vineland II corroborates these scores with an overall score of 74. In addition to all of these measures, the team spends significant time reviewing work samples, classroom observation records, and teacher reports focusing on Tomi's adaptive and cognitive functioning, particularly in his ESOL class.

In our policy summary (see www.tesol.org/lexceptionalneeds), we reviewed the historical mistreatment of people with disabilities, as well as the challenges faced by immigrants and minority populations as they try to navigate the United States school system. The history of the assessment of English learners has been less than kind to this particular group of students. For decades, unilateral decisions about how and where to place students from underrepresented populations were often based on uninformed judgments with little supporting data. These decisions, which often led to inappropriate placements for English learners with disabilities, were rooted in inconsistent special education laws across the states; this inconsistency remained the case until the mid-1970s.

In this chapter, you will gain a greater understanding of several key court cases that spawned change regarding the assessment and identification of English learners with (and in some cases without) disabilities. With a specific focus on high-incidence disabilities, you will learn more about the Individuals with Disabilities Education Act of 1990 (IDEA) provision regarding unbiased testing procedures; you will develop a greater understanding of formal assessment tools used in the special education identification process and how the language barrier is addressed in such situations; you will learn the legal timelines regarding assessment; and finally, through the eyes of a young man named Tomi, you will see the assessment process actualized for a student with an intellectual disability.

Historical Context

Early use of Intelligence Quotient (IQ) tests. In 1916, the first Intelligence Quotient (IQ) test was introduced in the United States by a Stanford psychologist named Lewis Terman. Terman's IQ test was a modification of Alfred Binet's original IQ measure and was accordingly named the Stanford-Binet. During World War I, IQ tests were at first seen as a logical way to measure the aptitude of recruited soldiers to match them with suitable military roles. However, by the mid-1930s, IQ tests were often used at immigration entry points, such as Ellis Island, to "examine" immigrants who wished to make their home in the United States. Unfortunately, IQ tests were used to make sweeping generalizations about certain groups of people. By the mid-1960s, these "groups of people" included children in school who were suspected of having an ID.

Diana v. California State Board of Education (1970). Prior to the case of *Diana v. California State Board of Education*, English was the sole language used to administer IQ tests. IQ test questions not only heavily depended on verbal responses, but many questions were also culturally biased. Students not raised in a typical white, middle-class family were more likely to have a difficult time successfully answering the assessment items. This overreliance on IQ tests led to many schools inaccurately placing students in special education programs.

This biased form of IQ testing set the stage for the case of *Diana v. California State Board of Education*. Diana and eight other students were determined to have

ID and were placed in special education programs. The IQ test administered to draw this conclusion was conducted in English, even though the primary language of all nine students was Spanish. This case challenged the use of English-only IQ tests to determine the placement of students in special education. Diana's family and lawyers demanded a retest of Diana and her peers in their dominant language.

Ultimately, the court ruled in Diana's favor, and all nine students were reassessed in Spanish. Not surprisingly, Diana scored considerably higher on her second IQ test. The court ruled that, in the state of California, testing administrators must test students in their dominant language or use a nonverbal assessment (one for which pictures and manipulatives may be used exclusively). Other Mexican American students already determined to have intellectual disabilities were also entitled to reassessment based on the outcome of Diana's case.

> So what is an example of a "biased testing item," you may ask? Consider a test where the following four pictures are presented to a child: a dryer, a dishwasher, a lawnmower, and a hairdryer. Suppose the evaluator posed the challenge: "Which one do we use to dry our clothes?" Children from a lower socioeconomic status (SES) may have never seen a dryer or a dishwasher. It's also likely that English learners not raised in mainstream America may not come from a home where luxuries like appliances abound. Finally, even English learners familiar with these appliances may be confused by the semantic similarity between "dryer" and "hairdryer" and the relatively nuanced distinctions between clothes dryers, dishwashers (which both wash and dry dishes), and hairdryers.

As a result of this case, a bit of headway was made for English learners: 1) states developed and standardized IQ tests that could be administered in other languages, and 2) currently, IDEA requires that all students be assessed in their primary language (the language "normally used by the child," 34 CFR, § 303.25) or using sections of tests that do not depend on knowledge of English.

Guadalupe v. Tempe School District (1972). Shortly after Diana's case, parents of elementary school children of Mexican American or Yaqui Indian background desired bilingual and bicultural education for non-English speaking students in the Tempe School District (TSD) in Arizona. Initially, the court determined that the district was fulfilling its responsibilities to students in the Guadalupe community, as TSD provided services to help cure "mental deficiencies" in students with English language difficulties (Tyler, 1997). Under Title VI of the Civil Rights Act of 1964, the school was not required to provide non-English speaking students with bilingual instruction taught by bilingual teachers.

However, the court ultimately ruled that the district did not provide the students with adequate instruction that would yield long-term competency in reading, writing, and language comprehension in both Spanish and English. It also determined the district should have provided instruction about the history of the parents and relatives of the students from these backgrounds but failed to do so. The case of the Guadalupe community emphasizes two key points: 1) although all bilingual programs are not alike, each program should be created with the intention of reducing the disadvantages of ethnic and racial minorities, and 2) the study of the history and culture associated with the student's primary language is considered an integral part of bilingual education.

The Modern-Day Assessment Process

In 1975, parents of children with disabilities rejoiced as a unified landmark law was passed that finally guaranteed the right to education for children with disabilities. P.L. 94-142, originally named the Education for Handicapped Children Act (EHA, 1975), has gone through multiple iterations, the most significant of which is likely its 1990 reauthorization, which changed the name to the Individuals with Disabilities Education Act. As you learned in chapter 3, IDEA is driven by six key provisions, one of which is a student's right to nondiscriminatory and multidisciplinary assessment. This section will expand upon the assessment provision, and you will develop a greater understanding of both the formal and informal assessment processes in special education, with specific regard to English learners.

Formal evaluation. The Individuals with Disabilities Education Act of 1975, 1990, and 2004 mandates that school teams evaluate any child with a suspected educational disability, including the following groups of children:

- Children attending private elementary schools, private secondary schools, and charter schools within the physical boundaries of the school system
- Highly mobile/transient children
- Migrant children
- Homeless children
- Wards of the state
- Children who are suspected of having a disability even though they may be advancing from grade to grade

A chart of all federal disability codes is presented in Table 1.

Table 1 Federal Disability Codes Under the Individuals with Disabilities Education Improvement Act (IDEIA, 2004)

1	*Intellectual Disabilities (ID)	Significantly sub-average general intellectual functioning, existing concurrently [at the same time] with deficits in adaptive behavior and manifested during the developmental period, that adversely affects a child's educational performance.
2	Hearing Impairment (HI)	An impairment in hearing, whether permanent or fluctuating, that adversely affects a child's educational performance but is not included under the definition of "deafness."
3	Deafness	A hearing impairment so severe that a child is impaired in processing linguistic information through hearing, with or without amplification, which adversely affects a child's educational performance.
4	Speech or Language Impairment (SLI)	A communication disorder such as stuttering, impaired articulation, a language impairment, or a voice impairment that adversely affects a child's educational performance.
5	Visual Impairment Including Blindness	An impairment in vision that, even with correction, adversely affects a child's educational performance. The term includes both partial sight and blindness.
6	Emotional Disturbance (ED)	A condition exhibiting one or more of the following characteristics over a long period of time and to a marked degree that adversely affects a child's educational performance: (a) An inability to learn that cannot be explained by intellectual, sensory, or health factors. (b) An inability to build or maintain satisfactory interpersonal relationships with peers and teachers. (c) Inappropriate types of behavior or feelings under normal circumstances. (d) A general pervasive mood of unhappiness or depression. (e) A tendency to develop physical symptoms or fears associated with personal or school problems. The term includes schizophrenia. The term does not apply to children who are socially maladjusted, unless it is determined that they have an emotional disturbance.
7	Orthopedic Impairment (OI)	A severe orthopedic impairment that adversely affects a child's educational performance. The term includes impairments caused by a congenital anomaly (e.g., clubfoot, absence of some member, etc.), impairments caused by disease (e.g., poliomyelitis, bone tuberculosis, etc.), and impairments from other causes (e.g., cerebral palsy, amputations, and fractures or burns that cause contractures).

(continued on next page)

Table 1 *(continued)*

8	Other Health Impairment (OHI)	Presenting with limited strength, vitality, or alertness, including a heightened alertness to environmental stimuli, that results in limited alertness with respect to the educational environment, that— (a) is due to chronic or acute health problems such as asthma, attention deficit disorder or attention deficit hyperactivity disorder, diabetes, epilepsy, a heart condition, hemophilia, lead poisoning, leukemia, nephritis, rheumatic fever, sickle cell anemia, and Tourette syndrome; and (b) adversely affects a child's educational performance
9	Specific Learning Disability (SLD)	A disorder in one or more of the basic psychological processes involved in understanding or in using language, spoken or written, that may manifest itself in an imperfect ability to listen, think, speak, read, write, spell, or to do mathematical calculations. The term includes such conditions as perceptual disabilities, brain injury, minimal brain dysfunction, dyslexia, and developmental aphasia. The term does not include learning problems that are primarily the result of visual, hearing, or motor disabilities; of intellectual disability; of emotional disturbance; or of environmental, cultural, or economic disadvantage.
10	Multiple Disabilities	Concomitant [simultaneous] impairments (such as mental retardation-blindness, mental retardation-orthopedic impairment, etc.), the combination of which causes such severe educational needs that they cannot be accommodated in a special education program solely for one of the impairments. The term does not include deaf-blindness.
11	Deaf-Blindness	Concomitant [simultaneous] hearing and visual impairments, the combination of which causes such severe communication and other developmental and educational needs that they cannot be accommodated in special education programs solely for children with deafness or children with blindness.
12	Traumatic Brain Injury (TBI)	An acquired injury to the brain caused by an external physical force, resulting in total or partial functional disability or psychosocial impairment, or both, that adversely affects a child's educational performance. The term applies to open or closed head injuries resulting in impairments in one or more areas, such as cognition; language; memory; attention; reasoning; abstract thinking; judgment; problem-solving; sensory, perceptual, and motor abilities; psychosocial behavior; physical functions; information processing; and speech. The term does not include brain injuries that are congenital or degenerative, or brain injuries induced by birth trauma.

(continued on next page)

Table 1 *(continued)*

13	Autism	Developmental disability significantly affecting verbal and nonverbal communication and social interaction, generally evident before age three, which adversely affects educational performance. Characteristics often associated with autism are engaging in repetitive activities and stereotyped movements, resistance to changes in daily routines or the environment, and unusual responses to sensory experiences. *(The term autism does not apply if the child's educational performance is adversely affected primarily because the child has emotional disturbance.)*
14	Developmental Delay (DD)	For children from birth to age three (under IDEA Part C) and children from ages three through nine (under IDEA Part B), the term developmental delay, as defined by each State, means a delay in one or more of the following areas: physical development; cognitive development; communication; social or emotional development; or adaptive [behavioral] development. States may also choose to include children who exhibit atypical development or behavior, or who are diagnosed with a physical or mental condition that has a high probability of resulting in a delay.

*Prior to 2010, the federal disability code, "Intellectual Disabilities" (ID), was termed "Mental Retardation" (MR). Rosa's Law (PL 111-256), referred to in chapter 3, stipulates that any and all usage of MR be replaced with ID.

Part B of IDEA states that any child between the ages of 3 and 21 is entitled to receive a full battery of testing, free of charge, related to the suspected disability. IDEA makes distinctions between the first time a student is evaluated (initial assessment) and any subsequent formal evaluations (reevaluation). You will see these terms again in the next section, so it is important to remember that some differences exist between the two.

Nondiscriminatory and multidisciplinary assessment.

Multidisciplinary. Although the term *nondiscriminatory* appears first in the IDEA language, the multidisciplinary piece of this provision is easier to explain and will therefore be addressed first. Simply defined, *multidisciplinary* means "across disciplines." Multidisciplinary assessment occurs when professionals from different (yet relevant and

> One issue with implications for English learners involves trauma. Current research indicates trauma, including adverse childhood experiences, can have significant impact on mental health and physical health, in childhood and well into adulthood. For refugee children, in particular, experiences can influence both their mental health and their cognitive learning (Henley & Robinson, 2011; Heptinstall, Sethna, & Taylor, 2004; Kaplan et al., 2016), and increasingly, schools have begun to put interventions in place to support students experiencing trauma (Kataoka S., Langley A. K., Wong, M., Baweja, S., & Stein, B. D., 2012), even if they are not formally evaluated or diagnosed.

complimentary) disciplines take part in the assessment process to gather, share, and evaluate a student in their area(s) of concern. Following is a list of professionals who may comprise such a multidisciplinary educational team:

- Special educator
- General educator
- ESOL teacher
- Psychologist
- Speech and language pathologist (SLP)
- Physical therapist (PT)
- Occupational therapist (OT)
- Audiologist
- Teacher for the deaf and hard of hearing
- Vision teacher/therapist
- Adapted physical education (APE) teacher
- Social worker
- School nurse
- Assistive technology specialist

You may be wondering, "How do I know who to involve if I suspect that one of my students has a disability?" This will be explained a bit later in this chapter under the focus area regarding the student evaluation plan (SEP).

Nondiscriminatory. This tenet of IDEA is a bit trickier to explain. The labeling and placement of students with disabilities in educational programs requires the use of nondiscriminatory assessment. This means that all states must

- Test students in their native or primary language. Language dominance testing must be conducted if there are any questions regarding which language is the student's strongest (most dominant).
- Use valid tests and evaluation procedures selected and administered to prevent cultural or racial discrimination.
- Validate the use of the assessment tools for the purposes for which they are being used.
- Utilize several pieces of information collected by a multidisciplinary team.

Tools available in Spanish. As stated above, IDEA mandates that students be tested in their native or primary languages, but the actualization of this process can be quite challenging for many school teams. In recent years, researchers and publishing teams have worked hard to create formal testing instruments available in

Spanish. While some of these instruments are merely Spanish versions of English assessments, other tools are actually normed (meaning that they were validated and tested with) on a group of Spanish-speaking children. In some cases, completely separate "sister" versions have been created in Spanish. See Table 2 for a sampling of common formal assessment tools used in US public schools; this table includes

Table 2 **Sampling of Formal Assessment Tools Available in Spanish**

Instrument	Ages	Norming Information	Developmental Area/Domain Addressed	Notable Highlights
BASC-III (Behavior Assessment System for Children, 3rd ed.)	2:0–21:11 (Teacher/Parent Rating Scales); 6:0 through college age (Self Report of Personality/SRP)	English Norms	Behavioral/ Emotional	Includes RTI monitoring for Tiers 2 and 3 Useful in diagnosing ED
**CELF-4 Spanish (Clincial Evaluation of Language Fundamentals)	5:0–21:11	Content specifically developed for a diverse range of Spanish speakers—not a translation of the English edition	Receptive and Expressive Language	Addresses semantics, morphology, syntax, pragmatics, and conversational skills Can be particularly useful in diagnosis of ASD
*DIAL-4 (Developmental Indicators for the Assessment of Learning, 4th ed.)	2:6–5:11	Spanish Norms	Motor, Language, Concepts, Self-help, Social development.	Includes "Speed DIAL" screening component Aids in assessment of developmental delay (DD).
*PLS-5 Spanish (Preschool Language Scale, 5th ed.)	Birth–7:11	Normed with 1,150 monolingual and bilingual Spanish-speaking children in the United States and Puerto Rico	Auditory Comprehension, Expressive Communication, Total Language	Ideal for children who are preverbal or have limited expressive skills.
PDDST-II (Pervasive Developmental Disorders Screening Test, 2nd. ed.)	1–4	English Norms	Screen for autism spectrum disorders (ASD)	Helps distinguish ASD from other developmental disorders

(continued on next page)

Table 2 *(continued)*

Instrument	Ages	Norming Information	Developmental Area/Domain Addressed	Notable Highlights
PPVT-4 (Peabody Picture Vocabulary Test, 4th ed.)	2:6–100	(Completely separate Spanish "sister" test—see below)	Receptive Language	Picture-based assessment; no reading or writing required Ideal for children who are nonverbal and/or have motoric needs that make speaking difficult
Test de Vocabulario en Imagenes Peabody (TVIP)	2:6–17:11	Norms are available for both Mexican and Puerto Rican standardization samples (combined norms available as well).	Receptive Language	Contains over 100 translated items to assess the vocabulary of Spanish-speaking and bilingual students Based on an older version of the PPVT (PPVT-II)
Vineland II (Vineland Adaptive Behavior Scales, 2nd ed.)	3:0–21:11	English Norms	Adaptive Behavior	Aids in diagnosis of: ID, ASD, attention deficit/hyperactivity disorder (ADHD), TBI, and hearing impairment
(WJ-IV) Woodcock Johnson Tests of Achievement, 4th ed.	2:6–90	Completely separate "sister" tool (see below)	Academic Achievement: Reading, Written Language, Math, Academic Knowledge	The Oral Language battery (set of subtests) can aid in the determination of English (and Spanish) language proficiency. The OL battery can yield a more complete reading, writing, or dyslexia evaluation (key for diagnosing SLD).
Woodcock-Munoz Language Survey-R Normative Update	2:6–90	Normed on both ELs and English proficient children	Reading, Writing, Listening, Language, Comprehension	Provides a Cognitive Academic Language Proficiency Score (CALP) ranging from 1 to 6

*Assessment tools for early childhood/preschool population with *some* overlap into early "school-age"; ** Separate early childhood instrument available. Compiled from Pearson Clinical Solutions (2018), Blatchley & Lau (2010), Dunn & Dunn (2007), Dunn et al. (1986), Schrank et al. (2010), Schrank (2014).

norming procedures, developmental areas addressed, and appropriate ages for which the instruments are suitable. (Of course, this list is not exhaustive, and, in the assessment process, no "right" instrument exists for all children, particularly English learners. Therefore, the fact that an assessment appears on this list does not mean it will be valid for every English learner, or even for most.)

Since the majority of the English learner population in our country speaks Spanish, the Spanish instruments referenced here represent a logical step toward assessing students in a way that circumvents the language barrier and yields robust and valid results. During the 2014–2015 school year, approximately 77% of English learners in the United States identified Spanish as their primary language (US Department of Education, 2016). So you're likely thinking: "What about students in our country who speak languages other than Spanish?" After Spanish, the most commonly spoken languages in order of frequency from most to least are Arabic, Chinese, Vietnamese, Hmong, Somali, Russian, Haitian/Haitian Creole, Tagalog, and Korean (US Department of Education, 2016). However, this list is certainly not comprehensive, as some school systems, particularly urban ones, report over 100 different languages spoken (NYC DOE, 2013; DCPS, 2018).

Considerations for all nonnative speakers. As you may imagine, standardizing a formal instrument with a new sample of the population requires a great deal of time, effort, and funding; thus, it is not feasible for test developers to create 100 different formal assessment tools to represent the collective languages spoken in our country's schools. So, what can be done in cases where a student speaks a very rare language and requires a complete a battery of testing? And what are the "rules" in this situation? There are no easy answers to these questions.

Each and every student must be assessed in their native or primary language. If formal instruments such as the ones listed in Table 2 are not available in said language, schools must, by law, find an interpreter to help with the administration of these assessments. Accurate interpretation during the assessment process is highly critical as students navigate testing items. Thus, school teams must take extra steps to ensure that any interpreter is equally proficient in English and a student's native language (Artiles & Ortiz, 2002). A high-quality interpreter can help school teams better understand a student's native culture, its potential to influence the how a student attempts to answer a question, and the culture's bearing on the answer itself (Blatchley & Lau, 2010). Please see Figure 1 for practical guidance regarding the use of interpreters.

_____ Try to avoid using family members unless absolutely necessary. Family members or close friends may unknowingly and unintentionally help the student answer questions. The presence of family members may alter the student's otherwise typical testing behavior.

_____ Research the language and any dialectical variations to ensure that you are hiring an interpreter who speaks the correct language. (For example, natives of Uruguay and Argentina speak Rioplatense Spanish, while natives of Chile speak a very unique [and difficult] Chilean Spanish. People in Cuba, Puerto Rico, and the Dominican Republic speak a dialect known as Caribbean Spanish.) The Chinese language also includes many dialectical variations.

_____ Consider the interpreter's experience with children. Although a particular interpreter may have worked well in the past to translate for parents during an individual educational plan (IEP) meeting, all interpreters are not necessarily created equal in terms of being "child friendly."

_____ Work with the interpreter ahead of time to ensure that acronyms and any vocabulary specific to the testing instrument are explained and understood.

_____ **Be sure to allow extra time for the actual translation processes that may occur during the testing session.**

Additional Considerations for Using a Proxy Examiner

If you are considering training the interpreter to be an ancillary examiner (someone who actually administers some assessments or assists in administration, in addition to simply interpreting what you say, please take note of the following items:

_____ Consult all manuals that accompany your testing instruments. Some testing tools, such as the WJ-IV, have specific guidelines for training ancillary examiners. (Other tools may strongly advise against this due to the specificity of training involved for the instrument.)

_____ For each and every testing session, make sure that at least one member of the child's IEP team is present to help establish rapport between the interpreter and the child.

_____ At least one school team member (preferably the key evaluator for the particular test) should observe the interpreter to ensure that cues are not given, administration instructions are adhered to, and the interpreter and student are interacting appropriately (Langdon, Castilleja, & Rhein, 2008).

_____ After the evaluation, the interpreter and evaluator should discuss the session, including student responses, language samples, and appropriateness of grammar, syntax, and phonology (Langdon et al., 2008).

Figure 1: Interpreters: Best practices checklist

Initial Evaluation and the Student Evaluation Plan (SEP). Under IDEA, school teams must first develop a student evaluation plan (SEP) in conjunction with the student's family. This plan cannot be implemented until at least one parent consents (via signature) to the evaluation process. The SEP must note any developmental areas of concern, decide which school-based provider(s) will be responsible for the testing in that particular developmental area/domain, and specify which assessment tools will be administered to best ascertain a valid picture of the student's abilities and needs. Potential developmental areas may include the following (this list presupposes that teams are considering the impact of language proficiency, both social and academic, as well as acculturation in assessing each of these areas):

- Academic performance
- Communication
- General intelligence
- Overall health, including hearing and vision
- Motor abilities (fine and gross motor)
- Social, emotional, and behavioral history

From the date of signed consent for an initial evaluation, the school team has 60 days to conduct the evaluation as outlined in the SEP, compile results, and bring the parents back into school for a second meeting to discuss results. If the student meets the criteria for an educational disability (see Table 1), the team then meets to draft an appropriate individualized educational plan. Although the student's new IEP may be approved by all parties during the assessment results meeting, school teams often need to bring the parents back in for a third meeting, a process that can be complex. While it is certainly in the best interests of the child to implement an IEP as soon as possible, it is also in the best interests of the child to carefully craft and not rush the IEP. Regardless of how teams decide to parse out the tasks related to IEP development, the student's IEP team must meet within 30 days of the assessment results meeting; after that, the new IEP must be implemented as soon as possible.

Reevaluation. As per IDEA guidelines, a student with a documented educational disability receiving services must be reevaluated (at a minimum) every three years. At this point, the IEP team, which always includes the student's parent or parents, will meet for a reevaluation meeting to decide what types of evaluation data should be gathered. Just as teams must do for initial assessments, the IEP team must create a new SEP; from the date on which the SEP is signed, the school team has 90 days to complete the process and reconvene with the student's family to present results.

At this juncture in our chapter, it is important to distinguish between the terms *evaluation* and *assessment*. *Evaluation* can be viewed as an "umbrella" term; the components of the evaluation umbrella include formal assessment results, informal assessment data, and other anecdotal records. Let's revisit the story of our friend Tomi.

Tomiwa's Triennial

Flash forward three years, and Tomiwa's family is now prepared to sit down with the school team for his SEP meeting; it's time to talk about his triennial reevaluation. At the meeting, the parents tell the school team that they would like them to refrain from doing any type of formal assessments, including IQ testing. However, they would like the team to gather as much informal assessment data as they can. They would also like the speech and language pathologist to complete new language dominance testing to see if Tomi is more proficient in English or Yoruba. Thus, the school team—though evaluating Tomi—may not actually be conducting many formal assessments.

This scenario highlights the distinction between the terms *evaluation* and *assessment* and also demonstrates several other issues important to culturally and linguistically diverse (CLD) families during the evaluation process. For many families, a low IQ score is extremely hard to digest and accept, particularly when its validity is questionable to begin with. Although individual IQ scores can vary a bit between administration sessions, research shows that they remain relatively consistent over time. Families often do not want to put their children through unnecessary testing only to see their scores stay the same and the intellectual disabilities remain. It seems that Tomi's parents want the team to gather data through informal methods to focus more on what he is doing and can do as opposed to focusing on a stagnant IQ score. According to IDEA, parents have the final say regarding which specific instruments, if any, will be used to assess their children. As you have read, school teams cannot begin assessing until the SEP is signed. Parents also have the right to revoke their consent to the testing process and can do so at any time during the 60- or 90-day window. School teams must gain signed permission for any testing that would not otherwise be given to a student. For example, the Dynamic Indicators of Basic Literacy Skills (DIBELS) measures or the World-Class Instructional Design and Assessment (WIDA), if given to whole classes of students, would not fall under the purview of permission-based assessment because they are not administered individually to just one student.

High-Incidence Disabilities

As you might be able to infer from the term itself, high-incidence disabilities are those most likely to occur in the student population. In 2015, students with specific learning disabilities (SLD) comprised roughly 35% of all students served under Part B of IDEA (NCES, 2017). The next most common disability categories include speech or language impairments (20%), other health impairments (12%), autism (9%), followed by developmental delay and intellectual disability, both of which present with a 6% incidence rate (NCES, 2017). The National Center for Education Statistics (2017) also reported a 5% incidence rate for children with an emotional disturbance (ED).

The number of students with autism spectrum disorders (ASD), while traditionally classified as low incidence, has increased in recent years, perhaps as a result of improved assessment and early intervention (Cole & Shapiro, 2005). For that reason, ASD will be considered high-incidence disabilities. Currently, many practitioners are "on the fence" about whether intellectual disability and emotional disturbance are high- or low-incidence disabilities. Using the NCES (2017) numbers as a guide, ID and ED will also be included as a high-incidence disabilities for the purposes of both the current and subsequent chapters.

Proceeding to eligibility determination for English learners who may have high-incidence disabilities requires schools and teams to have strong multi-tiered system of supports (MTSS) processes in place. For high-incidence disabilities, in particular, the judgment of assessors can play a significant role in determining whether a child is determined to have a disability and how significant that disability is determined to be (Patton, 2011; Hamayan et al., 2013). Teams should pay particular attention to the following elements.

Selecting assessments. Keeping in mind IDEA's provision that assessments be administered in the primary language of the child where feasible, teams should seek native-language assessments where possible (IDEA/IDEIA, 2004). Teams must also keep in mind that all assessments are biased and, indeed, educators' conception of school, assessment, and individual performance is itself based on a specific, culturally embedded, Western-specific model (Damico & Hamayan, 1991). Therefore, assessments should be selected to be appropriate for students' language strengths and needs and their cultural backgrounds. If substantial interpretation or translation are needed, consider whether the assessment as a whole is appropriate and necessary. See our assessment selection guide at www.tesol.org/exceptionalneeds for some questions for teams to consider in selecting assessments.

Administering assessments. Teams, including assessment personnel, should ensure assessments are administered in a manner that is culturally and linguistically appropriate and accessible. Some questions to consider about administration are found in the section "Accurately analyzing data," which follows the next section on potential bias.

Potential bias and the need for multiple assessment methods. As referenced above, assessments designed for English-speaking populations often assume students have a common set of experiences and background knowledge (Damico et al., 2013). These assessmentsmay also presume advanced language proficiency, making results invalid for students more fluent in other languages or whose background experiences and cultural frameworks differ from the norm (Hamayan et al., 2013). These factors place school personnel in difficult situations, particularly when assessing for high-incidence disabilities.

By law, assessment is a multidisciplinary process (IDEA/IDEIA, 2004), and assessment for high-incidence disabilities often involves consideration of factors such as academic performance and cognitive skill and behavior, areas with ample room for subjective interpretation and cultural influence (Bowen & Rude, 2006). Teachers may see academic performance as indicating a disability, when in fact it is a function of slower language processing, differing rates of fluency, or vocabulary development. Teachers may see unusual behavior as indicating a disability, when in fact it is a function of differing cultural expectations or experiences (see Bassam's story at www.tesol.org/exceptionalneeds, based on an actual incident at a US school).

Thus, teams often end up using a variety of assessments, some of which may be substantially limited for linguistic or cultural reasons. In such cases, it becomes important to triangulate information, utilizing multiple sources to develop a comprehensive and holistic picture of a student's functioning. Often, this may involve a greater reliance on informal, authentic, or classroom-based assessment than might be seen in assessing a native speaker of English. Assessment plans may involve consideration of performance-based assessments, curriculum-based measurement data, and authentic assessments as well as formal assessments. Assessment plans will likely also involve parent interviews or questionnaires, review of records from the home country or prior schools, review of health history, work sample analysis and classroom observations, and student interviews or questionnaires.

Accurately analyzing data. Teams should consider questions such as the following in analyzing the data they collect:

- Under what circumstances was this data collected?
- Can we assume these data are valid and reliable?
- Do these data represent the student's skills, motivation, and general performance?
- Is the student's performance in line with that of other English learners at the same grade and language proficiency level?
- Is the student's performance in line with that of other same-aged peers, including native speakers?
- Is it likely that language skills or understanding impacted the student's performance?
- Is it likely that cultural background and/or prior educational experiences impacted the student's performance?

A Tailored Assessment Approach for Ling

Ling is an energetic, fun-loving, and popular fourth-grade student from Korea. She joined her parents in the United States in kindergarten and mastered social English by first grade. She continued to demonstrate significant challenges with reading, writing, and math throughout elementary school despite participating in multiple intervention programs targeting these areas. Two of the interventions she received were bilingual or Korean-only. At the beginning of fourth grade, Ling's classroom teacher refers her for eligibility determination for special education services. The team's special educator, who happens to be a strong Korean speaker, works with the school and district ESOL staff to formulate a robust assessment plan for Ling, even though she had been exited from ESOL services in second grade. The team administers and reviews Korean and English versions of cognitive and academic tests. However, team members also recognize and discuss the fact that Ling might lack the fluency and automatic language processing needed to perform well on English-only tests, but she has little or no academic language in Korean, so the Korean-language tests might not be appropriate for her either. Therefore, the team creates an assessment plan in which team members consider formal, standardized data; data from Ling's last three interventions; work samples completed in both English and Korean; informal, classroom-based assessments (including several completed with the aid of a bilingual dictionary); and several detailed conversations. Interviews with Ling's family and review of her prior school records, her health inventory, and her medical records are all completed. By the end of the assessment process, teachers determined Ling did have an educational disability, specifically a learning disability.

Reviewing work samples. In reviewing work samples, teams should remain cognizant of the potential impact of language and culture, particularly in considering factors such as response time, use of written conventions, and literacy or oral language. An English learner, for example, may appear to have poor letter formation or pencil control, but this may in fact result from limited prior literacy experiences or unfamiliarity with writing conventions (particularly for students whose language is not alphabetic). Psychologists and related service providers, such as speech and language therapists, physical therapists, and occupational therapists, should be familiar with norms and contexts of the student's home culture. See the work sample review guide at www.tesol.org/exceptionalneeds for suggestions teams should consider when analyzing and reviewing student work.

Considerations for conducting interviews. A variety of resources exist for sample parent/family interviews. See the list of relevant protocols posted on our website at www.tesol.org/lexceptionalneeds. Many districts have protocols for conducting parent/family interviews, and some have protocols for student interviews as well (Breiseth, 2018; Freeman & Freeman, 2011; Kloosterman, 1999). While teams may find it best to adhere to their own district or school protocols for interviews, some overarching considerations should be integrated into planning and conducting interviews. These are briefly outlined here and are relevant to assessing students with low-incidence disabilities as well (discussed more fully in chapter 9):

- Is the interviewer fluent in the family's native language?
- Is the interview conducted face to face, in real time? If not, why? (Face-to-face interviews are preferable in terms of establishing rapport and being able to follow up on nonverbal and paraverbal cues.)
- Is the interview conducted at a convenient time and place for the family? Note that some families may not be comfortable coming to the school building, particularly parents who may not have legal documentation; others may be equally uncomfortable having school personnel come to their home.
- Does the interviewer take the time to establish rapport and communicate respect?
- Does the interviewer ask about the child's birth history, early childhood, health and development? If health care was provided in a dramatically different context, is the interviewer aware of that fact, and are the family members asked to elaborate?
- Has the interviewer made sure families understand all terms used in the interview?
- Does the interviewer ask about siblings, including their birth and health histories as well as academic histories?
- Does the interviewer ask about the child's use of home languages as well as English?
- Does the interviewer ask about the child's daily activities and interactions at home, including but not limited to homework completion?
- Does the interviewer ask about the family's, and the child's, involvement in community activities?
- Are other factors relevant to the child's suspected disability, and does the interviewer ask about them in a sensitive and clear manner?

Classroom observation. We recommend, if possible, observing students in the ESOL classroom as well as in the general education (or special education setting, for students undergoing reevaluation) setting. While district procedures and observation forms may differ across locations, age, and grade level, all classroom observation data should be reviewed in light of the following considerations:

- Was the class in English, the student's native language, or a combination?
- Were language-related supports and scaffolds provided? If so, what were they and did the student utilize them successfully?
- Was the content culturally appropriate and accessible? (For example, was the lesson on a topic that required extensive background knowledge the student might not have?)
- What classroom activities occurred? At any point may the activities not have been culturally appropriate or relevant? (For example, if the student's cultural background involved emphasis on collaboration and group communication, did the lesson focus only on individual learning, or were collaborative activities included as well?)
- Did the student participate in all instructional or assessment activities? If not, did the uncompleted activities require use of oral or written English?

Language proficiency and acculturation. Language proficiency data should be considered in the assessment process, for both high-incidence and low-incidence disabilities. For students suspected of having high-incidence disabilities such as learning disabilities or autism spectrum disorders, both of which impact language use and processing, data from the ESOL classroom may be particularly valuable. Additionally, teams should utilize the ESOL standards and curriculum to determine how accessible other assessment tools may be for the student.

Collier (2016) developed a tool widely used to provide a rapid snapshot of a student's level of acculturation, another factor that may substantially impact the validity of assessment results. The AQS (Acculturation Quick Screen) considers data about a student's living situation, social functioning, length of time, and language use, along with other variables, and it estimates a student's level of acculturation (Collier, 2016). This tool is particularly appropriate for students who have not lived in the United States (or their current country) since birth. When this screen determines a student has acculturated only slightly, particular caution should be used in interpreting assessments and drawing conclusions.

Dynamic assessment. One promising method of assessment, often utilized for speech and language assessment (but appropriate for other areas as well), is dynamic assessment. Developed in the tradition of twentieth-century research on learning and culture utilizing Vygotsky's (1978, 1979) theories of proximal development and learning, dynamic assessment involves conducting a baseline assessment, teaching a skill and/or strategy, and re-assessment (ASHA, 2018) (Vygotsky, 1979). This approach allows the testing professional to observe a student's ability to learn a skill, identify strategies, and generalize the skill or strategies during re-assessment. It also provides information directly relevant to future instruction (strategies that supported mastery; baseline and performance data related to classroom skills). Teams may benefit from the knowledge of dynamic assessment that their speech-language therapists, educational psychologists, and other members may bring. While it is unusual for dynamic assessment to be the primary data source, it can certainly play an important role. Particularly for English learners, a dynamic assessment approach allows teams to observe students' learning skills and—most important—customize learning to their languages and cognitive, academic, and socioemotional functioning.

Role of the ESOL Teacher

In determining the presence of disability as opposed to language or cultural difference, ESOL teachers play a critical role. It is likely that they will be experts in building on their students' language proficiency and perhaps levels of acculturation. Having a robust structure for collaboration across roles, as described in chapter 5, will certainly help teams to incorporate the ESOL teacher's input. Other suggested roles and activities for ESOL personnel are described here; teams may determine that input in one or more of these areas is needed.

- Reviewing assessments and providing input on language accessibility for a particular student
- Providing data to describe a student's performance (both academic and behavioral) in the ESOL classroom
- Consulting with teachers and teams to ensure linguistically appropriate interventions were implemented as part of tiered supports
- Providing input about appropriateness of potential future interventions
- Reviewing lessons and materials utilized while the student was being observed to provide observer with feedback on linguistic accessibility
- Providing guidance on parent communication, family background, and parent or family member interviews
- Helping to communicate with parents and family members or to conduct interviews
- Reviewing current or potential IEP goals to ensure they are linguistically and culturally appropriate

Eligibility Determination

At the end of the assessment process, team members should consider all the data to make an informed decision about whether the student likely has an educational disability or not. Unfortunately, no clear formula or protocol exist for doing so. Decision-making in this context sometimes requires teams to consider factors rarely present with native speakers of English. Nadine, a speech therapist administering assessments to a population that included immigrant and refugee children, noticed that about 50% of her students answered incorrectly on a vocabulary item asking them to distinguish between words such as "sadness" and "separation." After talking to students about their understanding of those words, consulting with colleagues, and considering students' backgrounds and experiences, she rescored the assessment with that item removed. In her formal report, she listed both the original and the revised scores and provided an explanation indicating that students' recent experiences and cultural backgrounds might have led them to make unusual associations between "sadness" and "separation."

A few general principles may guide teams in decision-making and determining eligibility. First, place greatest emphasis on assessments that are culturally and linguistically accessible. Second, for any assessment that does not appear to be culturally or linguistically accessible, attempt to gather complementary information in the same domain through classroom or informal assessment. For example, native-language and English work products might be used to supplement academic achievement test results. Third, remember that under IDEA, language cannot be the "primary cause of a student's difficulties." However, it can be an element (one among many) in a student's difficulties. Consider the totality of the data when determining which students have disabilities.

Summary and Conclusion

There is no "right" formula for multidisciplinary assessment of students who are English learners and who may have disabilities. This is the case for students with high-incidence disabilities and those with low-incidence disabilities as well, as you will see in the next chapter. Accurate, reliable, and sensitive assessment of English learners is, often, about learning to ask the right questions about students rather than assuming a static and inflexible assessment process will provide all the answers. Asking the right questions for, and about, these students often requires teams to think carefully about the students' language proficiency, cultural and family backgrounds, skills and cognitive backgrounds, and social or behavioral strengths and needs. Multiple measures, careful interpretation, and use of primary language assessments should all be considered in students' assessment plans.

Questions for Team Discussion or Shared Reflection

1. How does our assessment process (at the school or district level) address the needs of English learners?
2. In conducting formal assessment for English learners, do we consider informal and classroom-based assessment data in a meaningful way, with substantive consideration of language proficiency as part of this process?
3. Is our ESOL staff meaningfully involved in the assessment process for English learners, and if not, what is one concrete step our team can take to ensure ESOL personnel are involved going forward?

References

American Speech-Language-Hearing Association. (2018). Dynamic assessment, retrieved from https://www.asha.org/practice/multicultural/issues/Dynamic-Assessment

Artiles, A., & Ortiz, A., Eds. (2002). *English language learners with special education needs.* Washington, DC: Center for Applied Linguistics.

Blatchley, L. & Lau, M. (2010). Culturally Competent Assessment of English Language Learners for Special Education Services, Communiqué Handout, National Association of School Psychologists. Retrieved from http://www.nasponline.org

Bowen, S. K., & Rude, H. A. (2006). Assessment and students with disabilities: Issues and challenges with educational reform. *Rural Special Education Quarterly, 25*(3), 24–30. doi.org/10.1177/875687050602500304

Breiseth, L. (2018). *Getting to know your ELLs: Six steps for success.* Retrieved from http://www.colorincolorado.org/article/getting-know-your-ells-six-steps-success

Civil Rights Act of 1964, 42 U.S.C. § 2000d.

Collier, C. (2016). *Acculturation quick screen.* (3rd Ed.). Ferndale, WA: CrossCultural Developmental Education Services.

Cole, C. L., & Shapiro, E. S. (2005). Perceptions of trainers and practitioners regarding assessment and intervention for students with low incidence disabilities. *Psychology in the Schools, 42*(7), 677–689. doi:10.1002/pits.20118

Damico J., & Hamayan, E. (1991). Implementing appropriate assessment in the real world. In E. V. Hamayan & J. S. Damico (Eds.), *Limiting bias in the assessment of bilingual students* (pp. 303–318). Austin: Pro-Ed.

District of Columbia Public Schools. 2017. Supports for English learners. Retrieved from https://dcps.dc.gov/service/supports-english-learners-els

Dunn, L. M., & Dunn, D. M. (2007). *Peabody picture vocabulary test.* (4th ed.). Retrieved from https://www.pearsonclinical.com/language/products/100000501/peabody-picture-vocabulary-test-fourth-edition-ppvt-4.html#tab-details

Dunn, L. M., Lugo, D. E., Padilla, E. R., &, Dunn, L. M. (1986). *Test de vocabulario en imagenes peabody.* Retrieved from https://www.pearsonclinical.com/language/products/100000487/test-de-vocabulario-en-imagenes-peabody-tvip.html#tab-details

Education for All Handicapped Children Act of 1975, 20 U.S.C. § 1401 *et seq.*

Freeman, D., & Freeman, Y. (2011). *Between worlds: Access to second language acquisition (3rd Ed.).* Portsmouth, NH: Heinemann.

Hamayan, E., Marler, B. Sánchez-López, C., & Damico, J. (2013) *Special education considerations for English language learners: Delivering a continuum of services* (2nd ed.). Philadelphia: Caslon Publishing.

Henley, J., & Robinson, J. (2011). Mental health issues among refugee children and adolescents. *Clinical Psychologist, 15*(2), 51–62.

Heptinstall, E., Sethna, V., & Taylor, E. (2004). PTSD and depression in refugee children. *European Child & Adolescent Psychiatry, 13*(6), 373–380.

Individuals with Disabilities Education Act of 1990.

Individuals with Disabilities Education Improvement Act of 2004, 20 U.S.C. § 1400.

Kaplan, I., Valibhoy, M., Stolk, Y., Tucker, A., & Baker, J. 2016. Cognitive assessment of refugee children: Effects of trauma and new language acquisition. *Transcultural Psychiatry, 53*(1), 81–109.

Kataoka, S., Langley, A. K., Wong, M., Baweja, S., & Stein, B. D. (2012). Responding to students with PTSD in schools. *Child and Adolescent Psychiatric Clinics of North America, 21*(1), 119–133. doi:10.1016/j.chc.2011.08.009

Kloosterman, V. I. (1999). *Socio-cultural contexts for talent development: A qualitative study on high ability, Hispanic, bilingual students* (RM99142). Storrs, CT: The National Research Center on the Gifted and Talented, University of Connecticut.

Langdon, H., Castilleja, N., & Rhein, D. (2008). *Collaborating with interpreters/translators in assessing language disorders in EL students.* [PowerPoint presentation]. Annual Convention of the American Speech-Language-Hearing Association, Chicago, IL.

Patton, D. C. (2011). Evaluating the culturally relevant and responsive education professional development program at the elementary school level in the Los Angeles Unified School District. *Learning Disabilities: A Contemporary Journal, 9*(1), 71–107.

Pearson Clinical Solutions. (2018). Spanish Assessment and Intervention Solutions. Retrieved from Pearsonclinical.com/Spanish

Schrank, F. A., Wendling, B. J., Alvarado, C. G., & Woodcock, R. W. (2010). *Woodcock-Muñoz language survey–revised normative update (WMLS-R NU).* Retrieved from http://www.hmhco.com/hmh-assessments/bilingual/woodcock-munoz

Schrank, F. A. (2014). Introducing the Woodcock-Johnson® IV: The most comprehensive system for evaluating strengths and weaknesses among contemporary measures of achievement, oral language, and cognitive abilities. *Woodcock Johnson IV Preview, 1*, 1–11. Retrieved from https://www.hmhco.com/~/media/sites/home/hmh-assessments/clinical/woodcock-johnson/pdf/wjiv/wj_iv_author_newsletter_winter_2014.pdf?la=en

Tyler, Bryan J. (1997). *Guadalupe v. Tempe.* Retrieved from http://www.onenation.org/guadalupe.html

Vygotsky, L. S. (1978). *Mind in Society.* Cambridge, MA: Harvard University Press.

Vygotsky, L. (1979). Consciousness as a problem of psychology of behavior. *Soviet Psychology, 17*(4), 29–30.

US Department of Education, National Center for Education Statistics. (2016). Digest of education statistics, table 204.27. Retrieved from https://nces.ed.gov/programs/digest/d16/tables/dt16_204.27.asp

CHAPTER 9

ASSESSMENT AND IDENTIFICATION FOR ENGLISH LEARNERS: LOW-INCIDENCE DISABILITIES

AMY K. NOGGLE AND PATRICIA RICE DORAN

A Creative Assessment Approach for Paolo

Paolo, who is in third grade, was born with total hearing loss in one ear and only 20% hearing in the other. His family emigrated to the United States from Italy when he was 3 years old, and he has been receiving special education services ever since. Paolo has attended a specialized program for students who are deaf since entering the school system and uses American Sign Language (ASL) to communicate. His family taught him to read in Italian, although he does not generally have the opportunity to practice writing in Italian. Paolo receives ESOL support from an itinerant ESOL teacher, but she does not have training in working with deaf students or familiarity with Deaf culture, so her ability to connect with students at Paolo's school has been limited thus far.

This year, Paolo's case manager, Mr. Mandinach, is hoping to revise his individualized education program (IEP) to include greater emphasis on Paolo's native culture by including his family more in the process than they have been and to better integrate ESOL with Paolo's special education services. Mr. Mandinach schedules a meeting with Paolo's parents. Although they are generally able to understand and speak English, he arranges for an interpreter to be present to explain any specific educational terminology. He also speaks ahead of time with the personnel who work with Paolo, including his classroom teacher, speech therapist, and ESOL teacher. They identify ways to incorporate Italian culture and language into Paolo's daily work, and they are also able to leverage the school's flexible schedule to provide Paolo biweekly sessions in which the ESOL teacher is present for his ASL sessions. Mr. Mandinach remains concerned about the best way to assess Paolo's language, academic, and developmental functioning. Together with the ESOL teacher, speech therapist, and Paolo's family, he settles on a plan that includes assessment in ASL but also assessment of both Italian and English reading skills, with the ability to respond expressively (with constructed responses) in ASL and receptively (using multiple-choice questions) in English and Italian. The team also agrees to supplement formal and curriculum-based measurements with informal classroom data collected by Paolo's teachers, including participation logs, mastery on content logs, and self-assessments. As they leave the planning meeting, Mr. Mandinach breathes a sigh of relief. Finally, he feels, they will develop an accurate picture of Paolo's true skills.

In Chapter 8, we discussed educational disability determination and the formal evaluation process, with a particular focus on the robust assessment of English learners with high-incidence disabilities. In this chapter, we review the unique assessment challenges that arise when the worlds of low-incidence disabilities (LID) and second-language acquisition intersect. Current literature says little about how to best assess English learners with low-incidence disabilities. By examining several vignettes and understanding more about current assessment instruments, you will come away with new assessment strategies to use with this rare group of students.

General Considerations for Assessing English Learners With Low-Incidence Disabilities

Low-incidence disabilities are defined as those that typically affect less than 1% of the school-aged population (Jackson, 2011), though slight variations in incidence will obviously vary by specific disability. Students considered to have LID include those who are deaf or who are hard of hearing, those with low vision or blindness, those with deaf-blindness, those with traumatic brain injury, those with multiple and severe disabilities, those with physical or orthopedic impairments, and those with other health impairments (excluding students with attention deficit/hyperactivity disorder (ADHD), who form a high-incidence subgroup within that category). During the 2014–15 school year, children and youth with multiple disabilities, hearing impairments, or orthopedic impairments each accounted for 2% or less of those served under the Individuals with Disabilities Education Improvement Act of 2004 (IDEIA) (NCES, 2017). Children with visual impairments, traumatic brain injuries, or deaf-blindness each accounted for less than 0.5% of children served under IDEIA (NCES, 2017).

Challenges in Assessment of Low-Incidence Disabilities

Assessment of students who may have low-incidence disabilities presents multiple challenges to school personnel.

Shortage of knowledgeable personnel. First, personnel qualified in assessment and evaluation of various low-incidence conditions may be difficult to find at all, particularly in smaller or rural districts (Courtade, Shipman, & Williams, 2017). Rural schools constitute 27% of the nation's schools (NCES, 2016). Historically, rural schools tend to have fewer resources, present limited opportunities for professional development, and are typically farther away from colleges and universities (which may offer support in the form of student interns and research study opportunities) when compared to urban school systems. The demographics of rural schools continue to change due to increases in the numbers of families from culturally and linguistically diverse (CLD) backgrounds (Conroy, 2012). Sadly, rural schools experience some of the lowest teacher retention rates in the country; this concerning teacher attrition rate is compounded by the fact that special education teachers specifically are more likely to leave the K–12 workforce than teachers in other areas (Goldhaber, Krieg, Theobald, & Brown, 2015). Taken together, these factors present a quite a challenge for programs serving English learners who also have low-incidence disabilities.

Importance of specialized, interdisciplinary knowledge and skill sets. Second, those personnel who are available often have specialized knowledge related to the disability under consideration, but their knowledge in areas of cultural and language diversity may be limited. ESOL personnel, who generally have strong skills in areas of culture and language, may have a working knowledge of more common disabilities such as learning differences or ADHD, but their awareness of adaptations and supports for low-incidence disabilities may be limited. This gap of knowledge and personnel is particularly relevant for rare diseases or health conditions with specific impacts, such as Tay-Sachs syndrome, Williams syndrome, Turner syndrome, pediatric autoimmune neuropsychiatric disorders associated with streptococcal infections (PANDAS), and others, which may even lie outside the purview of most special educators.

Need for appropriate assessment procedures. A third challenge in assessing English learners who may have low-incidence disabilities is the need for appropriate assessment procedures, which can vary widely based on the disability and its impact on functioning (including language acquisition). For example, assessment for a young English learner with significant motor challenges will need to be individualized to compensate for the unavailability of expressive language, reading, and tactile or physical assessments. Assessment procedures may also be influenced by the cultural framework of the student and family, including whether they perceive the student as having a disability and what interventions or adaptations they see as culturally appropriate. A student with a complex seizure disorder, for example, may come from a cultural background in which seizures are a sign of divine favor rather than pathology; this background will almost certainly impact the family's approach to identification, remediation, and treatment. A family from an orthodox religious background may express strong beliefs about acceptable and unacceptable medical treatments based on their religious beliefs; while these beliefs will not impact educational services per se, the treatment path chosen by the family may have significant impact on the student's overall functioning and eventual outcomes.

Strategies and Approaches for Effective Assessment

In chapter 8, we emphasized that all areas of suspected disability must be tested by the multidisciplinary team. On our website, www.tesol.org/exceptionalneeds, you can review the assessment planning process utilized by the multidisciplinary team serving Luis, a 6-year-old English learner.

Children with LID are supported by educational teams that often comprise a number of related services personnel. When administering assessments, it is important to consult such professionals to ascertain what accommodations may be useful to the student while not jeopardizing the fidelity of the assessment administered. Related services providers may be able to help with accommodations during testing even if a certain test doesn't seem to "be the responsibility" of a certain provider. See continued discussion of Luis's assessment process at www.tesol.org/exceptionalneeds.

Assistive Technology

The assistive technology (AT) assessment, though an important consideration for all students with suspected or documented disabilities, is likely one of the most critical evaluations for students with LID. Historically, students with low-incidence disabilities have been placed in highly restrictive placements (Kurth, Morningstar, & Kozleski, 2015), thus minimizing their opportunities for access to meaningful interaction with same-age typically developing peers. Assistive technology, when matched explicitly to each child's needs and implemented with fidelity, has the potential to create autonomy and independence that may not be realized otherwise.

Related services professionals, such as speech and language pathologists (SLPs') and occupational therapists (OTs), may also be particularly helpful in conducting an assistive technology assessment. This assessment process, along with commonly used frameworks, will be described in the following sections as we attempt to answer these key questions:

- What are the benefits of AT?
- What steps do IEP teams take to decide if a child needs an AT device?
- Must all AT be computerized?

- What are the different classifications of AT devices?
- What kinds of tools are available to assist in the AT evaluation?

Definitions and legal foundation. An assistive technology device is "any item, piece of equipment, or product system, whether acquired commercially off the shelf, modified, or customized, that is used to increase, maintain, or improve functional capabilities of a child with a disability" (IDEIA, 2004, 602.1A).

As mentioned earlier, assistive technology has roots in both Section 504 of the Rehabilitation Act of 1973 and the IDEA. Children with disabilities are also afforded the rights to assistive technology under several other key laws:

- 1988: Congress passed the Technology Related Assistance for Individuals with Disabilities Act (PL 100-407) to increase access to, availability of, and funding for assistive technology for all individuals with disabilities, including very young children.
- 1994: This act was reauthorized (PL 103-218).
- 1998: Congress enacted the Assistive Technology Act (PL 105-394), and, in 2004, the AT Act was amended once again as PL 108-364.

Amendments to IDEA (1990) first introduced the terms *assistive technology device* and *assistive technology service*. Accompanying federal regulations (34 CFR § 300.105, 1990) stated: "AT devices and services must be made available to any child with a disability, if required as a part of the child's special education, related services, or supplementary aids and services." The only exception to this payment rule pertains to surgically implanted devices, such as a cochlear implant for a child with a hearing impairment.

IDEA stipulates that school teams must evaluate a student's need for assistive technology devices and services *each year* during the annual review of the student's IEP. (Note from chapter 8 that "evaluate" does not necessarily mean "assess.") If the team determines that the student should be assessed, this becomes part of the student evaluation plan (SEP). Subsequently, if the student qualifies, assistive technology must be provided by the school district at no cost to the family (34 CFR § 300.105, 1990). When implemented with fidelity, AT can provide the following benefits for English learners with disabilities: increased access to the curriculum, increased participation, increased independence, and increased confidence and competence. Please see www.tesol.org/exceptionalneeds for a sequential list of the steps involved in the AT assessment process.

Demystification of assistive technology. One of the most common myths surrounding AT is that it is only relevant for students with low-incidence disabilities. This is certainly not the case, as students with high-incidence disabilities, such as specific learning disabilities (SLD), may benefit from voice-to-text technology or graphic organizers, as examples, to aid in the writing process. In fact, AT use is often relegated to narrow populations such as elementary school students with specific learning disabilities (Bouck, 2016). As a professional community, educators need to work harder to investigate AT opportunities for English learners with low-incidence disabilities. To further minimize the mystery that often surrounds AT, is also important to address several other myths:

All AT is computer based and complex. Although some types of AT are certainly computer-based and complex, many "low-tech" options exist. These low-tech options, such as an adapted pencil grip, are often inexpensive and fairly easy to acquire. Assistive technology devices are conceptualized along a commonly accepted continuum ranging from low to high.

AT is the same as augmentative and alternative communication (AAC). This is not true, though the two are related and in some cases overlap. The goal of AAC is to improve the communication skills of individuals who have little to no functional speech (Lloyd, Fruller, & Arvidson, 1997). Remember that AT is defined as *any item* that supports a child's ability to participate actively in their home, child-care program, school, or other community setting; thus, the core difference between AT and AAC is that AAC is concerned specifically with a person's expressive communication. As part of an assistive technology evaluation, it may be determined that a student could benefit from an AAC aid or device. The American-Speech-Hearing Association (ASHA) defines an AAC system as a group of communication-enhancing components, which ". . . include forms of AAC (aided or unaided), symbols, selection techniques, and strategies" (ASHA, 2018). Please see www.tesol.org/exceptionalneeds for ASHA's list of possible AAC tools; you will notice that the three different categories of AAC (No Tech, Low/Light-Tech, and High Tech) are very similar to those used to classify AT.

AT solves all problems. AT certainly doesn't solve all problems, but it can level the playing field for children with disabilities. As school teams work to consider the needs of English learners with low-incidence disabilities, AT may be especially useful in reducing the "double whammy" experienced by these students.

Only AT specialists work with children to determine the need for AT. Evaluating a child's need for AT is the responsibility of the school team; as we reviewed earlier in this chapter, this team must be multidisciplinary. As part of the AT evaluation, all areas of the child's development must be considered. You may not find an assistive technology specialist in every school. Although some school systems (especially those in urban areas and/or those with more resources) may employ multiple assistive technology personnel, you may find that other school districts employ only one specialist, who must float from school to school. That said, the availability (or lack thereof) of an assistive technology specialist, or any related services provider for that matter, should never preclude 1) a fair and thorough evaluation of skills in all areas of suspected disability, 2) or the implementation of the student's IEP, which of course includes all related services.

The AT evaluation process. You are likely wondering, "How do I know where to get started with the AT process?" and "What diagnostic tools should my team use to conduct an assistive technology evaluation?" Since the passage of the first assistive technology law related to education (Technology-Related Assistance Act of 1988), practitioners and specialists have been working to create decision-making tools to aid teams in the comprehensive evaluation of a student's assistive technology needs. In the next section, you will learn about two of these tools. Please note that these are not formal testing protocols; rather, they are guiding frameworks meant to assist teams in the identification of appropriate AT services and devices.

Assistive technology frameworks

Student, Environments, Tasks, and Tools Framework (SETT). SETT (Zabala, 1995) is a four-pronged model designed to promote collaborative decision-making in all stages of the assistive technology evaluation and subsequent intervention. Although the SETT acronym is certainly catchy, it is not intended to imply order; rather, Zabala (1995) stresses that each of these components is just as important as the other. The SETT framework takes into consideration the "traditional" developmental domains (e.g., cognition, communication, social, physical, and academic). The tool also includes questions about other significant areas of the child's abilities and preferences including sensory, vocational, recreational/leisure, and finally, a construct called *environmental control*. The "SETT Scaffold for Consideration of AT Needs" is presented as Appendix 1. Although the SETT does not address English learners in particular, the framework does include questions about "continued barriers" (Zabala, 2005), which should certainly prompt teams to discuss any existing language barriers. If you are interested in additional documents related to this framework, you will find useful data collection forms and a decision-making checklist, among others aides, which can be downloaded free of charge directly from Joy Zabala's website (http://www.joyzabala.com).

Wisconsin Assistive Technology Initiative (WATI). WATI (2008) started as a grant-funded initiative designed to better enable schools in Wisconsin to meet the AT needs of its students (WATI, 2018). The culmination of this multiyear project is the WATI Assessment Package, which includes numerous tools and versatile checklists to help inform the AT assessment process. Similar to the SETT, the WATI's "Assistive

> You may now be thinking: "I am not sure about my own comfort level using technology in the classroom. Are there any tools that can help me?" The Technological Pedagogical Content Knowledge (TPACK) Framework offers guidance for practitioners regarding the implementation of AT in the classroom. TPACK is based on the premise that technology decisions should not occur in isolation, nor should an AT assessment be tacked onto an existing IEP as an addendum (Mishra & Koehler, 2006). The TPACK is unique in that it allows educators to align AT with curricular content as well as pedagogical approaches (Bouck, 2016). The TPACK is not a branded name belonging to any particular group of people; it represents a compilation of ideas that have evolved over time (Koehler, 2012).

Technology Consideration Guide" requires school teams to consider all areas of a child's development. (Please see Appendix 2 for a sample of this guide.) Though the content of both guides is quite similar, the WATI includes 13 specific "section" guides, each dedicated to a specific domain or skill set. Examples include motor aspects of writing, computer access, and mobility. The WATI also includes a section called "Activities of Daily Living" (or ADLs) aimed at addressing a student's functional skills (WATI, 2018). The WATI does not specifically address English learners in its language; however, its referral guide poses questions about both a student's and family's primary language. You can access free WATI forms at https://dpi.wi.gov/sped/educators/consultation/assistive-technology/wisconsin-assistive-technology-initiative/forms.

Considerations for Determining Educational Disability and Providing Services

Determining educational disabilitiy for students with low-incidence disabilities. As discussed in chapter 8, the determination of whether an educational disability exists can be nuanced and contextual. While a student's English learner status, or lack of prior instruction, cannot be the primary reason for a determination of disability, this does not exclude students who are English learners, or students with interrupted education, from being qualified for special education services. Teams should consider all relevant factors and use their judgment in determining the impact of language learner status or interrupted or inadequate former education.

For students with low-incidence disabilities, the discussion of whether impairment or disability exists is often clear-cut, as the disability may have been independently determined by a medical provider or social services agency long before the student entered school. Students with physical impairments, students who have low vision, students who are deaf or hard of hearing, and students with other health impairments may fit into this category. Eligibility determination will focus less on whether these students have a physical or cognitive impairment and more on whether that impairment significantly limits their functioning in the school environment and requires them to have individualized instruction.

Considerations for reevaluation. As required by the IDEA, students who have low-incidence disabilities should be reevaluated at least once every three years. This reevaluation should always take assistive technology needs, among many others, into consideration. In reevaluation processes for students with low-incidence disabilities, teams will consider existing data and determine what new information is needed to provide an updated picture of the students' current functioning, strengths, and needs. In doing so, teams should consider the impact of student growth, particularly with respect to language acquisition. In three years, significant changes are possible in an English learner's language use and fluency. Teams should discuss the extent to which any changes in language skills necessitate updated assessments or different programming or services. For example, a student who has exited ESOL may not need interpreters for assessment, and a student who has advanced several levels in ESOL may be able to access interventions or specialized instructional programs with more complex language than they had previously been provided. Last, a student who has not advanced in ESOL at all, over the space of several years, should be evaluated to determine whether services are truly meeting their needs.

Reevaluation for students with low-incidence disabilities, particularly English learners, will also consider the impact of any updated health information. If a student's health status has changed, if they have received a cochlear implant or other medical intervention, it is likely that their educational performance may have changed as well. Teams might also consider the extent to which any changes in family status, including immigration status or residence, have affected a student's day-to-day living situation or their ability to access services outside school.

Outreach to families of students with low-incidence disabilities. Families of students with low-incidence disabilities may be at risk of being doubly marginalized. Parenting a child with a significant or rare disability may contribute to feelings of isolation or frustration, and parents who are culturally or linguistically diverse themselves may experience difficulty accessing specific services or supports available to other parents. At the same time, the "funds of knowledge" model suggests that CLD families may be able to provide their children with strong familial and community support, even if this is not evident to members of the majority culture or language group. Outreach to CLD families of students with low-incidence disabilities can productively focus on honoring families' cultural perspectives about difference and disability, which may differ from those of the mainstream culture's. Outreach efforts can also focus on helping families to access community resources, such as clinics, support groups, respite care, and interpreters.

Summary and Conclusion

Assessment and eligibility determination for English learners with low-incidence disabilities requires teams to consider information about health status, prior education, and functioning in a variety of domains. Teams will likely integrate information from medical, speech, audiology, social service, and other records in determining the existence, nature, and extent of a student's disability. In chapter 10, we will review recommended practices for developing and implementing individualized programs for students with both low-incidence and high-incidence disabilities.

Questions for Team Discussion or Shared Reflection

1. What resources do we have available, at the school and at the district levels, to screen and assess English learners who may have low-incidence disabilities?
2. Are we, as a school community, adequately supporting and communicating with parents of students with low-incidence disabilities? How could we improve in this area?
3. What assistive technology solutions have we offered, or can we offer, to our English learners with disabilities, and have we made sure that technology is accessible to students from varying language and cultural backgrounds?

References

American Speech and Hearing Association (ASHA). (2018). Augmentative and alternative communication. Retrieved from https://www.asha.org/PRPSpecificTopic.aspx?folderid =8589942773&section=Key_Issues

Americans with Disabilities Act of 1990, 42 U.S.C. § 12101 *et seq.*

Assistive Technology Act of 2004, 29 U.S.C. § 3001 *et seq.*

Bouck, E. C. (2016). A national snapshot of assistive technology for students with disabilities. *Journal of Special Education Technology, 31*(1), 4–13.

Conroy, P. W. (2012). Collaborating with cultural and linguistically diverse families of students in rural schools who receive special education services. *Rural Special Education Quarterly, 31*(3), 20–24. doi:10.1177/875687051203100304

Courtade, G. R., Shipman, S. G., & Williams, R. (2017). Increasing academic rigor through comprehensive, ongoing professional development in rural special education: A description of the SPLASH program. *Rural Special Education Quarterly, 36,* 191–202. doi:10.1177/8756870517721900

Goldhaber, D, Krieg, J., Theobald, R., & Brown, N. (2015). Refueling the STEM and special education teacher pipelines: Colleges and policy makers have access to solutions that could reduce the shortage of STEM and special education teachers. *Phi Delta Kappan, 97*(4), 56–62. doi:/10.1177/0031721715619921

Individuals with Disabilities Education Act (IDEA, 1990), 34 CFR § 300.105.

Individuals with Disabilities Education Improvement Act (IDEIA, 2004), 20 U.S.C. § 1400.

Jackson, R. M. (2011). *Curriculum access for students with low-incidence disabilities: The promise of universal design for learning.* Retrieved from http://aem.cast.org/aem-center/about-aem-center.html#

Koehler, M. (2012). *TPACK explained: The seven components of TPACK.* Retrieved from http://tpack.org

Kurth, J. A., Morningstar, M. E., & Kozleski, E. B. (2015). The persistence of highly restrictive special education placements for students with low-incidence disabilities. *TASH, 39*(3), 227–239. doi:10.1177/1540796914555580

Lloyd, L. L., Fuller, D. R., & Arvidson, H. H. (1997). *Augmentative and Alternative Communication: A handbook of principles and practices.* Boston: Allyn and Bacon.

Mishra, P., & Koehler, M. J. (2006). Technological Pedagogical Content Knowledge: A framework for teacher knowledge. *Teachers College Record, 108*(6), 1017–1054. doi:10.1111/j.1467 -9620.2006.00684.x

Section 504 of the Rehabilitation Act of 1973, 29 U.S.C. § 794 *et seq.*

Technology-Related Assistance for Individuals with Disabilities Act of 1988, 29 U.S.C. § 2201 *et seq.*

US Department of Education, National Center for Education Statistics. (2016). Rural education in America. Retrieved from https://nces.ed.gov/surveys/ruraled

US Department of Education, National Center for Education Statistics. (2017). The condition of education: Children and youth with disabilities. Retrieved from https://nces.ed.gov/programs/coe/indicator_cgg.asp

Zabala, J. S. (1995). *The SETT framework: Critical areas to consider when making informed assistive technology decisions* (ERIC Document Reproduction Service No. ED381962). Houston, TX: Region IV Education Service Center.

Zabala, J. S. (2005). *SETT scaffold for consideration of AT needs.* Retrieved from http://www.joyzabala.com/uploads/Zabala_SETT_Scaffold_Consideration.pdf

Wisconsin Assistive Technology Initiative. (WATI, 2018). *AT tools and forms.* Retrieved from https://dpi.wi.gov/sped/educators/consultation/assistive-technology/wisconsin-assistive-technology-initiative

CHAPTER 10

INTENSIVE SUPPORTS AND SPECILIZED PROGRAMMING FOR ENGLISH LEARNERS

PATRICIA RICE DORAN AND GREGORY KNOLLMAN

Elena's Story: Resilience and Multifaceted Needs

Elena, a 12-year-old student in the fifth grade, was born in the United States but returned to her family's home country of Mexico when her biological mother died shortly after giving birth. She was raised there by a loving aunt and uncle, but when she was 6, she was seriously injured in a car accident, sustaining two broken legs and a severe brain injury. Following the injury, Elena experienced difficulty with simple physical activities such as walking, and she also suffered memory loss, post-traumatic flashbacks, and outbursts of rage. A year and a half later, her aunt and uncle brought her to the United States to seek better medical care. She was treated at a nationally known university hospital, where she received physical therapy and regained some of her physical abilities. After treatment, she was able to walk normally but still had difficulty with memory, rage, and post-traumatic stress disorder related to the accident. Although she attended a public, inclusive school, she required significant academic and behavioral accommodations as well as counseling services. Elena received ESOL services and has made slow progress as a result of her memory deficits. After 6 months, Elena's aunt and uncle made the difficult decision to overstay their temporary visas and remain in the United States with Elena so that she could continue accessing medical care and educational services. They consulted an immigration attorney for help in securing legal status, at least until Elena was of age, but the process went slowly. Now in fifth-grade, Elena is terrified that despite their efforts, her aunt and uncle will be deported. This constant fear, along with her cognitive and behavioral challenges and her continued slow progress in ESOL, make the academic and social demands of fifth grade feel overwhelming for her.

As described previously, intensive supports for students with significant needs—whether identified for special education services or not—typically involve more frequent and individualized interventions, along with specialized programming that is often formalized through an individualized education program (IEP) or 504 Plan. Planning and delivering such supports for English learners requires additional coordination to ensure that interventions are culturally and linguistically appropriate, that native language and culture are incorporated appropriately into short- and long-term planning, and that sufficient coordination of special education and ESOL or bilingual services will occur. Students' personal and family situations play an important role in planning as well and may drive team decisions about communication, interventions, and needed supports.

Additional care is often also required in identifying appropriate methods of progress monitoring and ongoing assessment. Last but not least, families of English learners may also require additional language support, and they may bring unique cultural, social, and religious perspectives that also influence how they view and participate in the special education process (Verdon, Wong, & McLeod, 2016).

Outreach to Families of English Learners with Disabilities

All of these considerations make it necessary for personnel, when creating and implementing IEPs or other intensive intervention plans for English learners, to take the time and effort needed to familiarize themselves with students' native languages, cultures, and family expectations and to form strong partnerships (Burr, Hass, & Ferriere, 2015; Rossetti, Sauer, Bui, & Ou, 2017). The ideas presented in prior chapters on responsive schools and family outreach are relevant here as well. Additionally, planning and service delivery for English learners require particular commitment to sustaining relationships with families (Rossetti, Sauer, Bui, & Ou, 2017). Elena's team members were sensitive to her family's concerns about legal status, taking the time to explain that their attendance at Elena's IEP meetings would not increase their risk of deportation as the school did not collect information about parents' residency or immigration status. In addition, team members made sure Elena had access to counseling services and included stress management strategies on her IEP as a way to support her in managing her ongoing anxiety.

The family communication guide found at www.tesol.org/exceptionalneeds provides ideas for team members to consider in working with families to design, provide and implement, and progress monitor for intensive supports. The story of

Lou (see www.tesol.org/exceptionalneeds) further illustrates how team members might consider the perspectives of both student and family members while also remaining true to their obligations under IDEA/IDEIA (2004).

In delivering individualized services to English learners and other diverse learners, school personnel also must engage in collaborative discussions with one another, as well as with families, to ensure they have identified efficient ways to integrate and coordinate services, including appropriately addressing students' cultural needs (Orosco & O'Connor, 2014). A planning guide for collaborative discussions is included at www.tesol.org/exceptionalneeds. Once strong collaboration is in place, planning for interventions and support becomes far more feasible.

Intensive Interventions and Supports

Beyond planning for family involvement and collaboration, planning for individualized interventions requires personnel to be aware of (among other things) appropriate intervention programs, models for productive coordination of services, and linguistically and culturally valid means of monitoring progress (Burr, Haas, & Ferrier, 2015).

Schools may utilize one or more models for specialized interventions and supports. As with targeted interventions, more intensive, individualized interventions are often (though not exclusively) delivered using pull-out services; they may also be provided within the general classroom setting through educator push-in, or integrated into instruction in an inclusive or self-contained classroom setting, often where a low student-to-teacher ratio is already present. The best method for delivering an intervention should be considered as carefully as (and may overlap with) questions of the student's overall placement.

In this chapter, we do not provide recommendations for specific models or interventions, as programs may change with each new edition and, more important, individual programs may or may not meet the needs of any particular student. Rather, we present some considerations for selecting and implementing culturally and linguistically appropriate interventions and supports.

Specialized supports for English learners must be selected with attention to students' native languages and levels of proficiency in all language. Sometimes teams assume that interventions must be provided in the language of instruction (most often English) or, alternatively, must be provided in a student's native language. Neither of these is universally the case. Rather, interventions should be provided in a language that the student can access and in a language that builds the necessary language, literacy, cognitive, or behavioral skills. A discussion of other considerations, such as literacy level and cultural fit, follows.

Providing supports in a language the student can access. As an absolute minimal criterion, all intervention or support must be linguistically accessible to the student. For students in the very early stages of learning English, this will often—though not always—require that an intervention be delivered in the student's native language. For students at more advanced levels of proficiency, the discussion is more nuanced. A student must be able to comprehend the vocabulary, syntax, and pragmatic context of the language used in the intervention. Any academic language must be comprehensible. For students who are advanced English learners, an intervention delivered entirely in English may satisfy all of these criteria. For students at intermediate levels of proficiency, the decision may hinge on a student's command of English, their routine use of the native language, the degree to which the student has literacy in the native language, and the student's command of academic language in both English and the native language. Some students may be English learners whose academic language is entirely in English; in this case, an intervention focused on specific technical terms would be appropriately delivered in English. The student's comfort level may also drive intervention selection, as learning may occur faster in a language that they know.

Finally, considering the language most accessible for the student involves awareness of the student's academic language, home language, and prior literacy in all languages. The student's grasp of academic language may be a factor; an intervention in Spanish might not be appropriate for a student whose phonics learning has all involved the US alphabet and orthographic system. Additionally, the language demands of the intervention must be appropriate to its intended outcome as well as to the student's background. For example, if an intervention is designed to improve a grasp of English vocabulary, an English language intervention is likely to be appropriate. If, however, an intervention is designed to improve overall literacy, social skills, or cognitive skills, it is very likely that a native-language intervention or one delivered in two (or more) languages would be most appropriate. For example, a reading comprehension intervention provided to a relatively early-stage English learner would most likely need to be delivered in both the native language and English. At a minimum, interventions provided in English to students who are not yet at advanced proficiency should include native-language support (Baca & Cervantes, 2004; National Academies of Sciences, Engineering, and Medicine, 2017), such as an English–native-language glossary, translation of concepts, and the opportunity to ask questions or discuss in the native language.

Considering the student's literacy level. Does the student have the literacy level to access the support provided? This is a critical question. In answering it, teams should consider the intervention's or program's general reading level (including Lexile level or other structured measures), along with features such as vocabulary, sentence length and complexity, and so on. If the student cannot read the material (content, directions, or both) without support, the intervention is unlikely to build new academic skills and promote remedial learning. This is the case whether the content under discussion is modified curriculum or takes the form of tools such as self-monitoring checklists or project planning guides. Language proficiency, native-language literacy, disability, affective considerations, or processing and executive functioning needs may impact literacy level.

Considering the student's cultural background. It may seem self-evident, but the cultural context of an intervention is paramount. Vocabulary interventions utilizing, for example, pictures of local fruits and vegetables may not be appropriate for a student unfamiliar with American crops. Even more important, the social context of an intervention can impact a student's ability to access the supports provided. An intervention delivered to a single student, involving processing on their own, may not be the best choice for a child whose culture stresses group decision-making and discussion. An intervention involving a competitive game is likely to be a poor fit for a child whose culture stresses cooperation over competition.

Considering the student's prior experience and schooling. Like all interventions, supports provided in Tier 3 (or higher tiers) must be a good fit for a student's prior experience, level of prior schooling, and academic needs. The example of Lan, on our website, demonstrates this principle (see www.tesol.org/exceptionalneeds).

Progress-monitoring considerations. As with targeted supports, selecting intensive supports also involves selecting appropriate methods to determine effectiveness. This calls for careful development of progress-monitoring strategies. In particular, any instrument used to monitor progress (such as a running record, a behavioral chart, or a classroom or curriculum-based assessment) must also be appropriate to the student's needs, language, culture, and literacy level. The example involving Ariana illustrates the importance of an appropriate progress-monitoring tool.

Monitoring Ariana's Progress

Ariana is a third-grader with an autism spectrum disorder. Her IEP calls for her to receive self-contained instruction in a specialized classroom for students with autism spectrum disorders, where she has access to increased sensory supports, specially designed instruction, and an environment with reduced distractions and intensive adult support. She also has an aide. She is an intermediate English learner and receives ESOL services in a pull-out setting three times a week. Her ESOL teacher is not trained in special education, although of course she has the support of her aide in ESOL as in other content classes. Ariana receives speech, occupational, and physical therapy and reading intervention, and she has a behavior support plan. Her reading intervention involves fluency and comprehension. Her reading teacher was using DIBEL S, a curriculum-based indicator of early literacy and learning skills, to measure her growth from week to week. Ariana's DIBELS scores remained largely unchanged over several months of intervention. However, at a monthly team meeting, the ESOL teacher pointed out that this assessment had not been normed on English learners, had few embedded sensory supports or accommodations, and presumed knowledge of English phonics, which Ariana is still developing. On further discussion, the reading teacher also realized she had not planned for a reliable way to measure comprehension. She suggested, instead, that the team conduct progress monitoring using a combination of DIBELS, authentic grade-level texts utilized in reading and ESOL classes, and texts in Spanish, Ariana's native language. These three measures, taken together, would allow the team to get a sense of how Ariana's fluency was developing. They further decided to monitor comprehension through a combination of native-language and English probes, which included multiple-choice questions, some expressive responses in both languages, and the opportunity to select and sequence pictures that represented the events in the story. Although the conversation at the meeting took much longer than team members had anticipated, everyone left feeling confident that they had a better plan in place to capture Ariana's growth.

The guide on our website (www.tesol.org/exceptionalneeds) provides teams with a quick-reference discussion aid for selecting appropriate supports and interventions.

Strategies for Developing IEPs

In addition to intensive interventions, students with intensive needs often require modified curricula and individualized plans, both of which are formalized in the individualized education program, a legal document described in our policy review (see online chapter 3 at www.tesol.org/exceptionalneeds). The IEP includes, but is not limited to, a statement on the child's present level of academic achievement and functional performance (PLAAFP) as well as current evaluation results. This information helps team members to make an informed decision about the program. Some of the components of an IEP document might include the setting in which the child will receive educational services, the accommodations or modifications that might be necessary to help the child within the general education curriculum, the special education and related services to be provided, and the educational goals that will best meet the needs of the child within their educational program. The process of developing an IEP should involve adequate time for input from multiple professionals, including those with expertise in language, culture, and other student-specific factors. The process should also allow for collaboration and feedback, sometimes leading to multiple drafts of the IEP or multiple meetings to resolve questions of placement, services, and accommodations. An IEP meeting can include a broad and often diverse group of people including but not limited to the parents, teachers, administrators, an educational psychologist, and the student. Further strategies are described here.

Be patient—allow for more time in developing and revising the IEP. Planning and implementing services for English learners who also have special education needs can be time-consuming, requiring consultation from multiple partners, review of records and information from different sources, and careful consideration of informal and progress-monitoring data. All of this takes time, particularly in school systems where team members may circulate among multiple schools or juggle multiple administrative responsibilities in addition to teaching. Federally mandated timelines for IEP development and implementation still apply. So too do timelines and requirements for annual review and reevaluation, and these need to be taken into account in the planning process. We recommend that teams plan extra time for assessment, identification and IEP development, annual review, and three-year reevaluation. Practically speaking, this may mean beginning assessment processes sooner than usual and scheduling annual review meetings well in advance. Scheduling assessments as early as possible allows time to coordinate with interpreters and analyze the data with extra care.

Schedule multiple meetings. More than once, we have encountered parents who begin the IEP meeting with a detailed—and often necessary—summary of their child: who she is, what his interests are, why it is critical for her to have a good education. For our English learners, all of this background information, touching on culture, language, and family situation, is particularly important. However, the standard IEP meeting lasts between 30 and 60 minutes and leaves no time for such discussion. For this reason, we recommend teams schedule a "get acquainted" meeting with parents prior to any formal IEP meetings. These are excellent opportunities to share background information, discuss current and potential needs, and establish shared goals and terminology. While it can be difficult to motivate teachers to show up to one more meeting, it is our experience that these "pre-meetings" often save time. Unlike IEP meetings, they can be conducted with most but not all team members, and they can occur virtually or by phone as well, although a face-to-face meeting is often preferable for establishing relationships.

Secure parent or family input in multiple ways, including face-to-face or phone conversations as well as questionnaires provided in advance of the meeting. As many ESOL teachers are aware already, parents of English learners may communicate best in other languages. They may also have demanding or inflexible schedules, and some parents who do not have legal documentation may prefer not to visit the school site or show identification fearing exposure to immigration enforcement (National Academies of Sciences, Engineering, and Medicine, 2017). Communicating the school's role (or lack thereof) in the immigration process can be helpful to these parents. In addition, teams should be flexible in their scheduling, offering parents options for meetings and making sure that parents know they can participate in a variety of ways and can request that a meeting be rescheduled. Sometimes, schools send official documents (such as the notification letter or the IEP itself) home in the native language but may neglect to translate follow-up or additional communications, such as reminder emails or informal communications from the team; teams should pay attention to language accessibility for all communications, whether formal or informal.

Consider coordination of services. Will the student receive ESOL support in addition to special education services? Will any services be provided by the general educator or ESOL teacher? Should the special educator and ESOL teacher plan to coordinate and collaborate regularly, and, if so, how will this coordination occur? Teams may often need to modify student schedules, class schedules, or provider schedules to facilitate coordination of services.

Consider language accessibility of goals and objectives. In addition to being age- and skill-appropriate, are goals and objectives appropriate in terms of the student's language proficiency? Will the student need additional ESOL accommodations, or native-language support, to attain the goals or objectives? If so, how will this be provided and how should it be reflected in the IEP? The reproducible planning guide found at our website (www.tesol.org/exceptionalneeds) allows teams to plan and evaluate the cultural and linguistic appropriateness of IEP goals.

Designing appropriate IEP goals is important for all learners, but particularly for those who are English learners. IEP goals must be 1) culturally appropriate; 2) linguistically accessible; 3) constructed to allow coordination between ESOL and special education to the extent necessary; and 4) appropriate to the student's age, development, skill level, and language proficiency.

Constructing Appropriate Goals for Andre

Andre is a 7-year-old English learner with Down syndrome. He was born in Senegal and has lived in the United States for two years. He receives ESOL services at a beginner level and is just beginning to use complex phrases and sentences. His receptive skills have improved in the past year, and he now understands and can follow two-step directions and multiclause sentences as long as the vocabulary is accessible to him. He receives speech and language services for an expressive language delay that impacts his articulation (pronunciation) as well as his speech fluency. He is just beginning to write letters and type with prompting. Andre's aunt, who is his primary caregiver, makes it a priority to keep in contact with his parents, who are back in Senegal. They FaceTime often, and she tries to take him back to Senegal once every year or 18 months. Because the journey is so long, Andre is typically out of school for several weeks when he goes.

Andre's IEP coordinator and special education teacher have very little experience working with English learners, so they turn to the ESOL teacher and the speech and language therapist for guidance. His special educator points out that, for many students on Andre's level, she would create a goal around social functioning, but she is unsure how to match developmentally appropriate social expectations with his language learning needs. She is also uncertain how to make sure his phonics and oral comprehension goals are written to take language comprehension into account. His existing goals, written last year by other team members who were also unfamiliar with ESOL, did not consider his ESOL status. Here are Andre's existing and new goals and objectives:

- **Goal:** Andre will improve written communication skills to grade level.

- **Sample objective:** Andre will utilize a graphic organizer or sentence starter to create a sentence describing his day.

- **New goal:** The team uses the goal planning tool provided in Figure 4 to create some more appropriate goals for Andre.

- **New goal:** Utilizing picture cues and oral rehearsal, Andre will communicate appropriately in writing to describe basic needs, questions, and information in English and Spanish.

- **New sample objective:** Utilizing picture sequence cards, a bilingual vocabulary sheet, and oral rehearsal in Spanish when needed, Andre will successfully create a declarative sentence, in English, with facts about his day.

Progress-monitoring considerations. As with targeted supports, progress monitoring for students with formalized IEPs should be carefully designed and carried out. Input from ESOL, school social workers or counselor, pupil personnel worker, and others is essential to strong social, emotional, linguistic, and cognitive planning. While progress monitoring is addressed more fully in chapters 5, 7, and 8, it is also an essential part of the process for intensive services and IEP implementation.

Role of the ESOL teacher. At many schools, ESOL and special education personnel may work alongside one another without explicit communication or a system for coordinating efforts. Such a bifurcation can make it difficult to serve students efficiently and well. We recommend that ESOL teachers be consulted in developing or implementing interventions for *any* student needing targeted or intensive support.

In addition, for students requiring IEPs, the ESOL teacher must be a team member. For students being assessed to determine eligibility, or for students receiving intensive supports who are not in special education, the ESOL teacher should nonetheless be a consistent part of the intervention and progress-monitoring team. The ESOL teacher's input can be invaluable in determining whether a student needs academic intervention at all (as opposed to language support), in facilitating bilingual or native-language intervention, in modifying materials for greater language accessibility, and in supporting progress monitoring by helping teams determine if a given instrument is valid for a given student.

How can one best allocate staff to effectively serve English learners with special education needs? Principals may struggle with the best pairing, best use of personnel, or (if they have hiring authority for the building), the best distribution of roles. Some models used with success involve assigning a resource teacher from ESOL and a resource teacher from special education to each grade to support planning and team meetings, or designating one class per grade as cotaught, with additional support available in that room. Some of our colleagues have worked in schools where principals created a de facto bilingual model by increasing class size to pair an English-speaking and Spanish-speaking teacher, allowing both to teach in their native languages. Building in scheduling flexibility, something possible with newer scheduling programs even in middle and high schools, provides more options for offering services to English learners with disabilities. ESOL and special education teachers can rotate into a given classroom together or can pull out for jointly delivered intervention sessions (such as, for example, a social skills session with language support embedded). Utilization of an effective scheduling system should also allow students to move between leveled classes throughout the day or week, rather than being tracked with the same group of students for convenience. Principals can increase support for English learners in the classroom by grouping lower-performing students with students who have a higher degree of language proficiency, allowing them to serve as a stronger resource.

Facilitating a Culture of Inclusion

Questions of inclusive practice go hand in hand with staffing. Some evidence suggests significant benefits for students (those with and those without disabilities) as well as teachers in schools that practice inclusion. Inclusive schools must align language supports, general curriculum supports, and disability-specific accommodations and adaptations (Baca & Cervantes, 2004; Abedi, 2014) to ensure that students are able to access, and succeed in, their grade-level curriculum. This may include social as well as academic success; inclusive planning for this group of students requires educators to consider all of the comprehensive supports needed to help students access grade-level social, emotional, academic, and language-related learning opportunities. See the example of Luis (carried over from chapter 9) at our website (www.tesol.org/exceptionalneeds).

To help schools avoid difficult situations, it is useful to reflect on the inclusion approaches they currently utilize. The team reflection tool provided at www.tesol.org/learnerswithdisabilities is designed to help teams review their own practices to identify areas for potential improvement (or for dissemination to other school systems as a model).

Additional Resources

You can use a number of additional resources to locate additional information about the rights and protections for individuals with disabilities and English learners. Several federal departments, agencies, and offices are dedicated to upholding the right to a free public education for this group of students in particular. See www.tesol.org/exceptionalneeds for descriptions of these agencies and offices, which frequently create and publish important guidance for educators working with English learners who have disabilities.

Summary and Conclusion

English learners with disabilities may be provided services in the general education setting, in a pull-out environment, in a resource room, or in a self-contained, more restrictive setting. Intensive supports and interventions for these learners must always be linguistically, as well as culturally, appropriate, with consideration given to their prior learning opportunities, current literacy, and levels of language proficiency to determine the best progress-monitoring strategies. This chapter presented several usable resources and self-evaluation forms for teams and schools.

Questions for Team Discussion or Shared Reflection

1. What is our model for supporting English learners with disabilities? Are services provided in the general education setting; if so, by whom? Are students pulled out of class for ESOL or special education services; if so, for how long?
2. What are relative strengths/weaknesses of this model?
3. How does our school involve parents in the IEP planning and implementation process? Could we improve in this area?
4. What percentage of our IEP goals would we estimate to be culturally and linguistically responsive? Are there ways for us to increase this percentage?

References

Abedi, J. (2014). English language learners with disabilities: Classification, assessment, and accommodation issues. *Journal of Applied Testing Technology, 10*(2), 1–30.

Baca, L. & Cervantes, H. (2004). *The bilingual special education interface.* Upper Saddle River, NJ: Pearson.

Burr, E., Haas, E., & Ferriere, K. (2015). *Identifying and supporting English learner students with learning disabilities: Key issues in the literature and state practice* (REL 2015–086). Retrieved from https://ies.ed.gov/ncee/edlabs/projects/project.asp?projectID=4483

Individuals with Disabilities Education Improvement Act. (2004). 20 U.S.C. § 1400.

National Academies of Sciences, Engineering, and Medicine. 2017. *Promoting the educational success of children and youth learning English: Promising futures.* https://doi.org/10.17226/24677

Orosco, M. J., & O'Connor, R. (2014). Culturally responsive instruction for English language learners with disabilities. *Journal of Learning Disabilities, 47*(6), 515–531.

Rossetti, Z., Sauer, J. S., Bui, O., & Ou, S. (2017). Developing collaborative partnerships with culturally and linguistically diverse families during the IEP process. *Teaching Exceptional Children, 49*(5), 328–338. doi:10.1177/0040059916680103

Verdon, S., Wong, S., & McLeod, S. (2016). Shared knowledge and mutual respect: Enhancing culturally competent practice through collaboration with families and communities. *Child Language Teaching & Therapy, 32*(2), 205–221.

CONCLUSION

In the introduction to this book, we shared our hope that the resources in each chapter would help educators to provide appropriate services and supports for English learners along the continuum of ability—from those with mild support needs to those who need far more intensive services. In each chapter, we have attempted to address the unique challenges that may face teachers serving English learners at risk for, or identified with, disabilities. As we stated at the outset, supporting this unique group of learners can be a complex process that involves careful decision-making over the course of weeks, months, and sometimes years. Supporting this group of learners also requires schools and educators to form caring and productive partnerships with families. Increasingly, ELs and their families may face unique challenges, which school staff must understand and address proactively and positively.

Additionally, new structures and processes for identifying students with disabilities in many districts mean that some students at risk academically or behaviorally may not immediately—or ever—be identified as having an educational disability. Rather, the focus in schools has shifted to ensuring an environment where all students can receive all needed services, regardless of label. We see this development as a positive one, reducing potential for inappropriate identification and increasing students' opportunities to receive timely support. However, the presence of inclusive and multitiered systems should never preclude teams from identifying a student when a disability is truly present.

We hope that this book will be used as a springboard for further discussion among school teams, for continued professional learning, and for effective identification and service delivery wherever English learners are served. In particular, we hope that our discussion of early intervention processes, including the use of universally designed and targeted supports in the general education setting, can provide educators with a renewed understanding of the options available to support English learners within inclusive settings. We also hope that the resources provided in the later chapters help teams struggling to implement unbiased assessment and identification processes and—most important—yield helpful information to classroom teachers. Effective instruction and intervention may or may not occur within the context of special education; in a well-structured process, it precedes identification and, indeed, continues throughout the process of assessment, evaluation, and identification.

That last concept, above all, we hope is of value to our readers. The assessment and identification processes, and indeed special education as a whole, are valuable not in and of themselves, but because they allow us to provide all children an exceptional and equitable education, which in turn prepares them to access opportunities throughout their lifetimes. Effective supports allow these students to be successful in P–12 classrooms. Furthermore, they serve as an avenue to equity, facilitating the continued success of all learners beyond P–12 classrooms—in universities and vocational programs, in corporate boardrooms, operating rooms, performing arts venues, small businesses, and wherever else their talents lead them. Appropriate services and special education support are an essential piece of that larger vision. And that vision, in turn, is part of the mission of education in general and inclusive education in particular: working to ensure all our students have the opportunity to discover and use their giftedness in powerful ways.